Mediterranean Tortoises

LANCE JEPSON
MA VetMB CBiol MIBiol MRCVS

Designed by David Downing
Printed in China through Printworks Int.Ltd

Contents

Mediterranean Tortoises

Mediterranean tortoises are popular, though increasingly rare, pets. They are certainly a challenging animal to keep successfully away from the warm, dry climate where they are an important and unique aspect of the local fauna. For many years, tortoises were "harvested" from the wild in vast numbers to supply the international pet trade. Fortunately, that bulk trade has now ended, although habitat destruction and illegal collecting continues to threaten surviving populations.

The bulk pet trade was particularly destructive, as the vast majority of tortoises taken in this manner were dead within two to three years as a result of poor husbandry and a lack of understanding of tortoises environmental needs. Breeding in captivity was virtually unknown, and if breeding did occur, the survival rate of hatchlings was very low due to incorrect nutritional management. Things have - thankfully - changed in that regard and today there is no reason why you cannot provide a pet tortoise with a long, healthy and happy life. Animals already in captivity can also provide the basis for sustainable future generations via captive breeding.

Two problems have continually assailed would-be tortoise keepers over the years: no information and incorrect information. Unfortunately many books (and today, Internet websites) propagate information which is misleading and inadequate. I am pleased to say that this book is very different. The information contained here is a sound basis for designing your husbandry program, and will help you to avoid the many pitfalls along the way. Pay particular attention to the chapters on nutritional management and environmental requirements, as these often cause confusion and can easily lead to major husbandry failures. Unfortunately, we continue to see sickly, deformed tortoises on a regular basis. This is very sad; as such problems are entirely avoidable if only keepers took the trouble to find good advice, and then followed it diligently. This book contains excellent advice; it is up to individual keepers to implement it!

Andy C. Highfield
Director, Tortoise Trust

Chapter One

HOW A TORTOISE WORKS

The shell is a defining feature of the tortoises and other chelonians

Tortoise anatomy is so unique that it often provokes questions as just to how it all fits together. In particular the shell is the problem - is it part of the tortoise, or does it just fit on to the tortoise, like a hermit crab slots into an empty shell? And how is everything arranged inside? To answer these and other questions we need to look objectively at both the anatomy and physiology of the tortoise - in other words how a tortoise works.

The Skeleton

The chelonian skeleton can be divided into four distinct sections:

The axial skeleton:
This is made up of the vertebrae, that form the backbone. This runs down the central line of the tortoise. Starting from the front there are eight neck vertebrae followed by ten dorsal vertebrae that are in contact with the shell along with their associated ribs. Next there are two sacral vertebrae that attach to the pelvis, and finally there are the tail vertebrae (25 to 30 in number). The neck part in particular is very flexible - when it pulls the head back into the shell it forms a vertical S-shaped flexure.

The appendicular skeleton:
These are the bits stuck on to the axial skeleton - namely the fore limbs, the pelvis and the hind limbs. Of interest is that tortoises

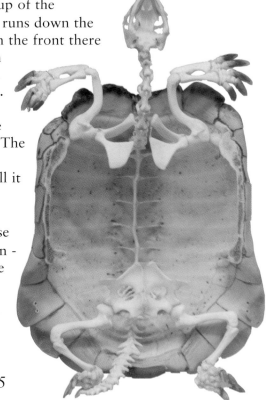

A Herman's tortoise *(T. hermanni)* skeleton with the plastron removed to show the bones of the backbone as well as the front and back legs.

5

and other chelonia are the only animals whose shoulder blades are on the inside of their rib cage!

The shell: This consists of 59 bony plates that are fused to the central few vertebrae and the pelvis. It encases all of the internal organs. The upper shell is called the carapace and the lower shell the plastron. The joints between the two halves on either side of the body are the plastrocarapacial bridges.

The skull: This houses the brain and the organs of special sense.

The main function of the skeleton is to prove a firm support from which the muscles work, in effect becoming levers. In chelonia the bones, particularly those of the shell, are important for protection and as a reservoir of calcium.

Skin

Skin of chelonia is of several kinds.
• Over the head, neck, upper forelimbs, tail and hind legs it has a leathery appearance. It is thick and tough with no obvious scaling. When this skin is shed, it does so piecemeal and not all at once like what we see in snakes.
• The lower front legs however are covered with large, tough scales. These scales act as protective shields when the

A Herman's tortoise with front legs clamped shut, demonstrating the protective role of the large scales on the front legs

head and front legs are drawn in, effectively sealing off the front of the shell. They are also used for digging and can be very abrasive when rubbed across unwelcome hands!
• Finally there are the scutes of the shell. These are modified scales and usually there are 54 in number. They are named according to their position (see diagrams (a) Carapace and (b) Plastron) Like other scales elsewhere on the body, these have an outer layer of keratin (a similar compound to our finger nails) that overlies a very thin skin layer, that in turn lies on top of the bone. The skin layers between the scutes are very thin and it is here that new keratin is produced. Unless worn away, this keratin is not shed like the rest of the skin, but is retained as characteristic rings. When tortoises are rapidly growing, these areas between the scutes often take on an obvious yellowish white lined appearance.

Diagrams: above (a) Carapace and below (b) Plastron

The Shell

The characteristic chelonian shell is therefore composed of a collection of bony plates covered by a number of keratinised scutes. The joints between these two sets rarely overlap thereby increasing the overall strength of the structure. In some species the plastron is hinged at the junction of the hypoplastron and xiphiplastral plates (which from the outside is between the abdominal and femoral scutes) forming a flap-like arrangement of the back-most section of the plastron. In some male species the plastron has a marked concavity of the abdominal scutes. This is a secondary sexual characteristic and is not present in every male. The shell is a marvellous evolutionary invention but as with all evolutionary experiments it is a trade off between its benefits and its downsides. Tortoises have a greatly reduced anatomical flexibility - as an example they cannot actively clean their back end, potentially leaving themselves open to parasitic fly or tick attack.

The Respiratory System

At the back of the tongue lies the glottis, which is the entrance to the trachea (windpipe). The trachea in tortoises is very long to allow for the flexibility of the neck, and it divides part way down sending a tube into each lung. The two lungs lie side by side and occupy the upper third of the space inside the shell. Unfortunately the body cavity cannot expand like ours in order for the tortoise to inhale, so instead it must shuttle air in and out of its lungs by squashing them with its other internal organs. This is done by pulling in the limbs so that the large muscle bodies at the top of the legs squeeze into the body cavity, or in those species with a hinged plastron, alternately lifting and releasing the caudal flap. Tortoises are very adept at surviving low oxygen levels, and this, combined with the position of their lungs, can enable them to survive traumatic events such as falling into garden ponds.

The Cardiovascular System

Tortoises have arteries and veins like other vertebrates. Unlike in the human heart, the tortoise heart is a three chambered structure with two atria and only one ventricle. However when the ventricle contracts there is a functional separation between the blood flow to the lungs and that to the rest of the body.

The Digestive System

Mediterranean tortoises are herbivores - a diet that causes some problems for them. Much of the plant material that is eaten is cellulose and no vertebrates, not even tortoises, produce the enzymes necessary to digest this material. They must therefore rely upon bacteria present in the bowel to break down cellulose into compounds that the tortoise can utilise. The whole of the digestive system is adapted to this end.

The tortoise jaw contains no teeth. The upper and lower jaws carry thin blades of keratin that act as shears, slicing through plant material. If this proves too tough then the front legs are brought into play, pulling the rest of the food

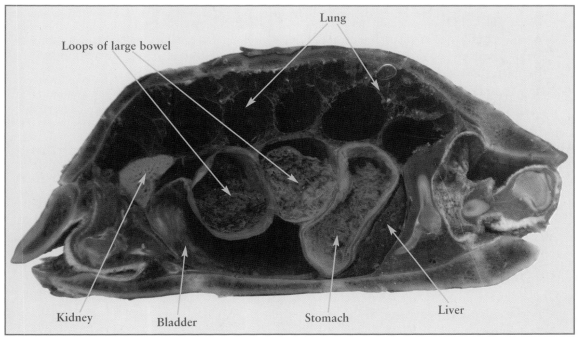

A cross-section through a Spur-thighted tortoise *(T. graeca)* showing the relative positions of the lungs, liver, bowel, bladder and kidney.

particle away from the body so that it tears. There is a large muscular tongue to help with this process as well, although it is not very mobile. Food is therefore cropped and swallowed in large chunks without much chewing. Ingested food travels down the oesophagus and into the stomach where digestion begins in this acidic environment. Over a period of time pieces of this food are released into the small intestine where some proteins and carbohydrates are digested, whilst the more indigestable parts are shipped and stored for bacterial fermentation in a modified large intestine.

Eventually much of this plant material is reduced to short chain fatty acids (acetate, butyrate and propionate) that are absorbed into the circulation and used as sources of energy.

In the wild this bacterial degradation may be aided by other naturally present organisms. Present in wild Spur-Thighed Tortoise *Testudo graeca* are populations of the oxyurid pinworms Tachygometria spp. There are eight distinct species of these worms and amazingly they form an ecological community in the gut of *T. graeca*. The different worm species are found in different parts of the large intestine, both linearly and radially (i.e. associated with either the middle or the gut lining). These species are probably beneficial to the reptile in the wild state, churning food material in the large intestine as well as breaking it down into smaller particles thereby aiding bacterial degradation, and it is highly probable that routine worming will eliminate them for the tortoise gut. It may be that inappropriate fibre levels tip the balance of these potentially beneficial organisms into pathogenic parasites.

It takes time for the plant material to be broken down. Food will reach the large intestine from the stomach within twelve hours, but it may be retained in the large bowel for up to four to six weeks.

The Liver is an extremely important organ, necessary for producing bile to help digest fats, detoxify toxins, make blood proteins and blood clotting agents to mention only a few of its functions.

The Urinary System

Reptiles excrete their metabolic waste nitrogen not as urea as we do, but as uric acid crystals - the white sand-like sludgy substance naturally present in their urine. This is because reptiles attempt to conserve water: by excreting uric acid as a sludge they need to lo se less water as urine than by eliminating it as urea, a substance that requires relatively large volumes of water in which to dissolve and to carry it. The kidneys are paired structures situated close to the pelvis. Urine is formed here and is drained down the ureters (small tubes) to the bladder, where it is stored. Unfortunately reptile kidneys

The white, gritty material found in tortoise urine is uric acid crystals.

cannot concentrate urine, so it is further concentrated by having water absorbed from it across the bladder wall or by refluxing some urine back into the large intestine. The tortoise bladder is a voluminous structure and can hold a significant volume of water. This is used as insurance in case the tortoise is unable to drink for a while, or it can be used as a distracting escape tactic as anyone who has had a tortoise urinate down them will testify.

The Reproductive Tract

Female tortoises possess two ovaries. Multiple follicles form on these ovaries from which eggs are ultimately formed. At the stage of ovulation they just look like egg-yolks and these pass into the oviducts. Further down the oviducts a

This female Herman's tortoise has a relatively large clitoris - something that can lead to confusion when sexing. To the left is one ovary freshly removed during her surgical ovaro-hysterectomy

calcium-rich shell is laid down around the egg. Female tortoises have special crypts close to the end of their reproductive tract that can store sperm for several years.

Male tortoises have two testes that lie close to the kidneys. They do not possess a true penis but instead have a phallus, which is an erectile organ in the cloaca that has a groove running down one side to allow sperm to be conducted during mating. The phallus is a large, almost mushroom-shaped structure that is often darkly coloured. Some males regularly protrude this organ and concerned owners regularly mistake this for an intestinal prolapse. The phallus plays no part in urination. Some female tortoises have a relatively large clitoris that can be easily mistaken for a phallus.

The Cloaca

Tortoises do not have separate external orifices for the urinogenital tract and bowel. The gut, bladder and reproductive tract all communicate into a chamber known as the cloaca. The lining of the cloaca can reabsorb moisture from faecal/urine mixtures to help conserve the reptile's water. This intermingling of excreta is largely why tortoises often produce urine and faeces at the same time.

A closer view of the toroise's head

The Endocrine System

This refers to the hormonal system and is as complex as that found in mammals. Hormones control many of the body's functions. Of note is the pineal gland that is sensitive to light and daylength and which produces melatonin, affecting both daily cycles and seasonal cycles such as hibernation.

The Nervous System

This is complex, and like with us, is composed of a brain, spinal cord and a peripheral nerve network.

Organs of Special Sense

Eyes

The eyes of Mediterranean tortoises are relatively large and their vision is good - in fact sight is probably their main sense. Their colour vision is also good as the retina is well supplied with colour sensitive cones. It is thought that tortoises can probably see in the ultraviolet spectrum.

Ears

Tortoises have two ears, set well back on the head and made obvious by the presence a of large tympanic scale covering each one. This scale is in the equivalent place to our eardrum. Each middle ear is connected to the inside of the mouth cavity by a small tube called the Eustachian tube.

Chemical Sense

Tortoises have three means of sensing food and other chemicals. These are olfaction (sense of smell) detected in the lining of the nose; gustation (taste) detected in the lining of the tongue and other oral surfaces; vomerolfaction detected in the lining of specialised vomeronasal organs situated in the roof of the mouth. Vomerolfaction picks up non-airborne scent particles from the tongue and lining of the mouth and may play a part not only in food detection but also individual recognition based on an individual's scent profile. This may apply as much to how the tortoise recognises you as it does to how it tells other tortoises apart.

Touch

Tortoises are 'sensitive' animals despite the fact they are built like minature armoured tanks, the skin and shell are well supplied with nerve endings that are sensitive to a number of stimuli such as touch, pain, heat, cold and so on. Particularly in female Herman's tortoises, touching the back half of the shell will trigger them to straighten their back legs and so raise their back end. This may be a reflex that would be triggered by pressure from a mounting male to help with mating.

Thermoregulation

Tortoises, as reptiles, are often inaccurately called 'cold-blooded'. This term refers to the fact that tortoises are unable to generate their own body heat unlike birds and mammals. However tortoises do regulate their own body temperature, using external heat sources to do so. Such animals are termed ectotherms. The main heat source is the sun and the tortoise warms up by basking in the sunshine until

Basking tortoises will often tilt their shell to alter their angle to the sun, thereby increasing or decreasing the surface area available for heat obsorption.

13

it reaches its Preferred Body Temperature (PBT), which for Mediterranean tortoises is around 30°C. The PBT is the temperature that the body of the tortoise works best at, including all of its internal chemical reactions, its digestion, immunity and its gut bacteria.

Most tortoises in the wild or in the garden will bask on a morning to warm up, and again during the late afternoon before seeking their place of rest for the

night. During the midday when temperatures are highest they will seek shade, whilst at other times of the day they will vary their thermoregulatory behaviour, fitting other essentials such as feeding and mating around attempts to keep their body temperature optimum. Hibernation is a means of opting out of difficult times in nature. For some Mediterranean

A male Spur thighed tortoise with old 'shell-rot' lesions happily basking in the borders of the garden.

tortoises it helps them get through periods of poor food availability. It is dealt with in more detail in Hibernation.

Longevity

Tortoises are long-lived creatures. Well documented ages of 80, 90 or 100 years plus are not uncommon. Ageing is, however, difficult. The growth rings seen on the scutes define only a period of growth that does not necessarily conform to one year's growth as seen with the growth rings of trees. Also in older tortoises that have been wild or allowed to live a feral existence in the garden, wear on the scutes occurs as a result from abrasion during digging or bacterial and fungal erosion, removing the earlier growth rings. In general an aged tortoise can be identified by the worn appearance of the scutes and the presence of a light coloured ring around the iris in each eye known as the arcus senelis. It is worth remembering that the European trade in Mediterranean tortoises (including that into Great Britain) was banned in 1984. Most adult tortoises alive today will have been pre-ban imports, and were quite possibly in their mid-twenties to thirties at that time.

Chapter Two

SPECIES DESCRIPTIONS

Mediterranean tortoises are all relatively closely related *Testudo* species that share a number of characteristics. A working knowledge of the different species and subspecies is important. It allows for an improved care of our tortoises by allowing us to modify our care methods to suit each specie. There is also increased emphasis placed on keeping single species groups as a means of reducing the risk of disease spread.

Spur-thighed Tortoise *(Testudo graeca)* Complex

The spur-thighed tortoise *(Testudo graeca)* is a species with a wide geographic range along the African Mediterranean region and into the Middle East. There appear to be many geographic races that are clearly distinguishable, and the situation becomes even more complicated when some of these races are so

Large female *Testudo graeca graeca*

different as to be considered as different subspecies, or even species. Hence the whole population of these tortoises is often referred to as a 'complex'. To apply order to a confused taxonomic situation is difficult but the following is derived largely from literature produced by Andrew Highfield of the Tortoise Trust.

Tortoises of this complex have also been introduced into a variety of new areas including the Canary Islands, France, Sardinia, Italy, and Sicily. Whether these introductions are from known geographic areas or are of mixed origin is unknown, but this would certainly further complicate matters.

Traditionally the species *Testudo graeca* has been divided into four subspecies:-
Testudo graeca graeca LINNAEUS 1758
Testudo graeca ibera PALLAS 1814

Large female *Testudo g. graeca* - note the rounded, shield-like first vertebral scute.

15

Testudo graeca terrestris FORSKAL 1775
Testudo graeca zarudnyi NIKOLSKI 1896

Re-assessment of original work and further detailed studies of tortoises
collected and studied in the wild has meant that the following tortoises would
now come under the umbrella of the 'complex'. These are:
Testudo graeca graeca LINNAEUS 1758
Testudo graeca terrestris FORSKAL 1775
Testudo (graeca) ibera PALLAS 1814
Testudo (graeca) zarudnyi NIKOLSKI 1896
Testudo whitei BENNET 1836
Testudo nabulensis HIGHFIELD & MARTIN 1989

In the interests of consistency, the
above nomenclature will be used
(although it has not been
agreed on by all authorities).
It is also worth noting that
the population known as
Libyan Greek tortoises
found in Cyrenacia in
Libya (formerly
considered a race of *T.
graeca*) has now been
renamed *Testudo cyrenacia*.
Testudo graeca terrestris appears
to be a dubiously defined species and may
prove to be a synonym for one or more as
yet poorly described species.

Adult female Libyian Greek tortoise now
renamed *Testudo cyrenacia*.

Testudo graeca graeca LINNAEUS 1758

Description
This tortoise is restricted to North Africa, primarily Libya, Tunisia and
Morocco. Many other tortoises have in the past been erroneously ascribed to
this species, leaving the true *T. g. graeca* a difficult species to categorise.

    T.g. graeca are generally small to medium sized tortoises. The background
colour to the carapace is generally a yellowish to yellow-green colour with dark
brown to black markings present on each of the carapace scutes. These
markings on the vertebral and costal scutes take the form of a central, large spot
with further markings present around the outside of the scute, in some cases
forming an almost ring-like appearance. The plastron is hinged between the
abdominal and femoral scutes. This is particularly obvious in adult females

where this hinge allows an increase in the space between the supracaudal scute and the floor of the plastron to facilitate egg-laying. The first vertebral scute is shield-like in appearance with rounded edges. The central marginal scutes have a fairly distinctive triangular marking. The supracaudal scute is single in the majority of individuals although a small percentage do carry a divided supracaudal scute. Two spurs are visible either side of the tail - one on each thigh and it is these

Moroccan *T.g. graeca* male

structures that give this tortoise its common name. They rarely extend beyond 2.5mm above the surface of the skin. There is a marked difference in body size between the sexes with adult females being considerably larger than males.

The races of this tortoise can be distinguished to some extent. The Libyan race (possibly now *Testudo cyrenacia*) has a very yellow background to the carapace with black markings on the scutes giving an almost leopard-like appearance. Moroccan specimens generally have a darker olive-green appearance with the scutes well marked. In Algerian T. g. graeca the carapace is a lighter yellowy-olive with reduced markings that are much less well defined.

Size
Adult females are usually around 150 to 190mm carapace length and weigh around 1.0 to 1.5kg. Males are correspondingly smaller - usually no bigger than 180mm and 1.0kg in weight. In the wild, adult size is achieved at 25 to 35 years after which growth slows down but does not cease altogether.

Temperament
Generally reasonably quiet with males not as aggressive as those of *T. ibera*. In households with both *T. graeca* and *T. ibera*, the graeca males are often seriously damaged by the aggressive activities of male ibera which can inflict serious shell damage by repeated ramming.

Sex Differences
Adult females are consistently significantly larger than males. Males also possess a longer and thicker tail, and a concavity of the plastron is usually visible in this sex.

Moroccan *T.g. graeca* male

Natural Habitat
Dryer, almost arid environments with seasonal flushes of plants. In the northern part of their range this species hibernates

17

during the colder spells, whilst in the warmer southern areas it will aestivate for the hottest months.

Testudo graeca ibera PALLAS 1814

Description

T.graeca ibera is considered by some to be a separate species *T. ibera*, rather than a subspecies of *T. graeca*. Their natural range includes north eastern Greece, Turkey, Iran, Iraq, Jordan and Syria, and going northward into Caucasus (Dagestan, Azerbaijan, Eastern Georgia and Armenia) i.e. they are not found naturally in North Africa.

Superficially this subspecies resembles *T.g.graeca*, but closer inspection reveals that the first frontal scute is angular, whereas that of *T.g.graeca* has curved edges. The posterior marginals are often flared to some extent. The carapace and plastron is often amber coloured, with the scutes having thick dark borders with a central spot on a yellowish centre. The head is quite robust and the eyes are large and prominent. The outward facing scales of the front legs are wide and rounded, whilst the claws are short, blunt and black.

Young 'Golden Greek' *T.g. graeca*. This lighter colour morph appears to occur naturally in some of the dryer, hotter areas of *T.g. graeca* distribution.

Relatively dark (melanistic) populations are to be found in the central Zagros Mountains of Iran, as well as Iraq and the extreme eastern part of Turkey (Highfield & Martin). Smaller, more yellowish individuals are found in southern Turkey and Syria.

Size

This is a large tortoise. Average carapace length in males is around 160 - 200mm, whilst females are slightly larger at 180 - 220mm

Temperament

This tortoise appears to tolerate the UK climate reasonably well, possibly because it occurs naturally in countries with environmental extremes. Males can be particularly aggressive towards other tortoises and regularly will do significant damage to males of other species.

18

Sex Differences
As described above, adult females are consistently larger than males. Males also possess a longer and thicker tail, and a concavity of the plastron is usually visible in this sex.

Natural Habitat
Dry scrubby areas. Will hibernate during colder periods.

Notes
Another putative *T. graeca* subspecies, *T. graeca nikolskii* has been suggested (Leontyeva and Demin 1995) for the population of *T. g. ibera* found at the north eastern (Caucaus) Black Sea Coast. It is very similar to *T. g. ibera* but there are some slight morphological differences. It is debatable whether this constitutes a new subspecies.

Adult female *T. g. ibera* - note the angular first vertebral scute.

References
Highfield A.C. and Martin J. A Revision of the Testudines of North Africa, Asia and Europe.Tortoise Trust Web Site

Leontyeva O.A. and Demin S.A. 1995 The Genesis of the isolated Testudo Graeca Nickolskii Area at the North Eastern Black Sea Coast in International Congress of Chelonian Conservation Proceedings

Testudo graeca terrestris FORSKAL 1775

Description
This is a small subspecies (carapace length up to 250mm but averaging 150mm) said to be present in Syria, Lebanon and Israel. Claims of its presence in Turkey appear to be ill founded. This appears to be a poorly defined subspecies that is said to be distinguishable from *T. g. graeca* by the high domed carapace and yellow markings on its head. The background colour to the carapace is light and a central

A small, aged male *T. graeca* typical of the form often referred to *Testudo graeca terrestris*

marking or spot is usually present. There are rarely any markings on the sides of the scutes as seen in other *T. graeca* subspecies. The head has obvious yellow markings on the forehead and sides.

It has to be said that the description and nomenclature of this tortoise does need to be addressed as it seems that accounts by different authors may be describing different, hitherto undefined species, particularly from Israel and Palestine. In view of the political situation there this needs to be addressed.

References
Highfield A.C. 1988 The status and nomenclature of Testudo (graeca) terrestris FORSKAL 1775: with additional notes on some little known land tortoises of Israel including Testudo floweri BODENHEIMER 1935. Tortoise Trust Website.

A second view of this same possible *T. g. terrestris*

Testudo graeca zarudnyi NIKOLSKI 1896

Description
This subspecies is found in Iran and neighbouring Baluchistan (Pakistan), although it appears to be quite rare throughout its range. This is potentially a relatively large tortoise. The carapace is elongate in outline with the hind-end border upturned to give a flared appearance, and is an olive-brown colour with little obvious patterning. The first (frontal) vertebral scute is often quite angular as seen in *T. ibera* as opposed to that seen in *T. g. graeca*. The fifth vertebral scute is not wider than the third in this tortoise. There are, however, noticeable diagonal reticulations on the vertebral and costal scutes. The marginal scutes at the front and

The Iranian Spur-thighed Tortoise (*Testudo graeca zarudnyi*)

back are often pointed with a translucent horny point to them. The plastron is dark with occasional lighter markings. The front legs are flattened and the covering scales are large and black - adaptations for burrowing. The skin of *T. g. zarudnyi* is a pale olive-brown. Eyes are almond-shaped.

Size
Adult females can readily weigh in excess of 3.5kg and a carapace length of over 280mm. Males are smaller.

Natural Habitat
Dry, inhospitable landscapes often on rocky hillsides and plains. Typically found at an altitude of between 1,000 and 2,500 metres.

Gilbert White's Tortoise *(Testudo whitei)* HIGHFIELD & MARTIN 1989

Description
Testudo whitei BENNET 1836 is found only in North Africa (Algeria) and is a large species. The background colour to the carapace is yellowish colour. The vertebral and costal scutes carry central brown to black markings but these are not so pronounced as with *T.graeca*. In some individuals they are absent. There is usually a distinct radiating pattern arising from the central growth points of the scutes on the vertebral and costal scutes. There are few, if any, of the triangular markings of the marginal scutes as seen in the true spur-thighed tortoise. If present they are not well defined. The dark markings on the plastron are darker and more diffuse than with *T. graeca*. The overall shape of the carapace is broader and flatter than the spur-thighed tortoise. The thigh spurs are large and often pointed and typically curl sideways towards the tail.

An adult female Gilbert White's Tortoise
(Testudo whitei)

Size
Adult females have, on average, a carapace length of 240 to 280mm and weigh

21

between 2.0 to 3.5kg. Males are smaller with a carapce length up to around 250mm and weights of around 2.0 to 2.5kg.

Temperament
Typical of the spur-thighed complex.

Sex Differences
Aside from the above mentioned size differences, males have a longer and thicker tail.

Natural Habitat
Little information is available on the natural habitat of *T. whitei*.

Testudo nabulensis
(HIGHFIELD & MARTIN 1989)

The Tunisian tortoise (*Testudo nabulensis*) is a small tortoise found in Tunisia only.

These tortoises have a carapace of a yellowish background colour with black markings on the scutes. Both vertebral and costal scutes have a central black marking. The vertebral scutes also usually have a dark border along the leading and side edges whilst on the costals there is colouring on the leading edge and variably on the other sides. The first costal in particular often lacks the leading border. The marginals have a dark border along the leading edges of the marginals and in some individuals these markings form triangular shapes. The plastron is not patterned other than having a large, poorly defined black marking in the central abdominal region. Two small thigh scales are present. These can be paired in some individuals.

A male Tunisian tortoise
(*Testudo nabulensis*)

Size
Males (carapace length up to 120mm) are much smaller than females (130mm+) and also have a much lower vaulted carapace than females. Maximum weight of females likely to be below 800g.

Temperament
These tortoises are relatively mild mannered although males will readily spar.

Their small size allows them to be kept more easily in vivaria and should not be subjected to hibernation except for relatively short, controlled spells.

Sex Differences
Obvious size differences between adults of different sexes. Again the tail is longer and thicker in males than that of females. The supracaudal scute in males is curved inwards. In females this scute is reduced in size and does not curl inwards.

Natural Habitat
Well vegetated grazing land or sunny, rocky verges of forests. Generally avoid arid sandy areas although there are coastal populations.

A male Tunisian tortoise (*Testudo nabulensis*)

References
Highfield, A.C. (1997) Tunisian Tortoise Description, Tortoise Trust Newsletter, Spring 1997.

Hermann's Tortoise *(Testudo hermanni)*

Description
There are two subspecies of Hermann's tortoises - the Western race *T. hermanni hermanni* and the Eastern race *T. hermanni boettgeri*. The main feature that distinguishes this tortoise from other Testudo species is the lack of spurs on the thigh areas and the presence of a spur-like scale at the tip of the tail. The shell is slightly flatter than those of the *T. graeca* complex. The presence of a divided supracaudal scute is a reasonably dependable but not always absolute criteria for identification (see subspecies descriptions). There is no hinge in the plastron.

The tail of a Herman's tortoise *(Testudo hermanni)* showing the characteristic spur-like scale at the tip of the tail.

Western Hermann's Tortoise *T. hermanni hermanni* GMELIN 1789.

This tortoise is naturally found in southern France, southern Spain, Italy and the Balearic islands. It is the smaller of the two subspecies with a carapace length rarely exceeding 165mm in males and 190mm in females.

The colour of the shell is of a background yellow colour with

very dark to black markings on the scutes. The last vertebral scute frequently has a well-defined, characteristic

Above: An old Western Hermann's Tortoise *T. hermanni hermanni*
Left: The Plastral markings

"keyhole" pattern and virtually all of this subspecies have a divided supracaudal scute. If the tortoise is turned over then the plastron markings are obviously of two thick, black strips running the length of the plastron, divided by a bright yellow central line. The head is relatively smooth and elongated - almost serpentine in appearance.

Eastern Herman's Tortoise *T. hermanni boettgeri* MOJSISOVICS 1889

The range of this subspecies is Greece, the Balkans and Turkey. There are also island populations on Corfu, Sicily and Sardinia. Possibly because of this range

An aged Eastern Tortoise *T. hermanni boettgeri*. Note the long standing lesion affecting the second vertebral scute.

there is a much greater geographic variation in appearance within this subspecies. Of the two races this is the larger with specimens readily exceeding 200mm carapace length, with females up to 300mm. The background colour of the shell is a greenish-yellow and the darker markings are not nearly so distinctly defined. Between 8 and 18% of Eastern Hermann's the supracaudal scute is not divided. The plastral markings are usually less distinct than those seen in Western race and are more variable in character. The head is shorter and thicker than that of the Western race.

Temperament
These tortoises are relatively placid and are quite cold hardy. A tolerance of damp conditions does mean that they are one of the species best suited to survive the climate of Great Britain.

The plastral markings of an Eastern Herman's Tortoise *T. hermanni boettgeri*.

Sex Differences
In adult Hermann's tortoises the main feature between the sexes is the length and size of the tail. In males the tail is very much longer than in females and is much broader at the base as it must contain the retractor muscle that allows the male to pull back the phallus internally following mating. Females, with no need for this apparatus, have a much shorter tail without the thickened base. Males are often significantly smaller than females and usually have a concavity of the plastron.

Natural Habitat
Hillsides and slopes with significant vegetation cover such as woodland and scrub with access to sunnier, more open areas for basking and egg-laying.

Note: A dwarf Sardinia form *T. hermanni sarda* has been described from southern Sardinia. It lives sympatrically with the dwarf form of the Marginated tortoise.

Egyptian Tortoise *(Testudo kleinmanni).*

This diminutive tortoise species is a native of northern Africa and was considered to range from Libya to Sinai. Recently this species has been subdivided into the true (a) ▪ Egyptian tortoise (*T. kleinmanni*) LORTET 1883, found west of the Nile and the (b) ▪ Negev tortoise (*T. werneri*), found east of the Nile.

This is a small tortoise. The carapace is usually coloured some shade of yellow and the vertebral scutes have the front and sides clearly defined in brown. There is no central spot to the scutes as seen in the T. graeca complex. In the vast majority of individuals the plastron bears two dark triangular markings on the abdominal scutes. The skin is pale yellow. There are no thigh tubercles.

Size
Males have a carapace length of around 90 to 100mm, whilst females are not much bigger at 120mm.

Temperament
These are relatively peaceful but can be quite active. Males are known for their unique cry during mating. Despite being a desert animal, the best background temperature range for this species is between 15 - 25°C. At temperatures above 30°C activity decreases in line with their normal behaviour of aestivation at high temperatures.

Sex Differences
Males have a longer tail than females with a more slit like opening to the cloaca.

Natural Habitat
These tortoises are found amongst the grasses and other vegetation that stabilise the desert sand dunes as well as other scrubby habitats.

Marginated Tortoises *(Testudo marginata)*

Generally considered to be the largest Mediterranean tortoise (with the possible exception of T. whitei), Testudo marginata SCHOEPFF 1792 also has the most limited range. Its natural range is southern Greece (from Mount Olympus southwards) although there are introduced populations in Sardinia and Tuscany. The carapace has an elongated shape to it and the caudal marginals are markedly flared. This flaring gives rise to its Latin name of marginata, meaning marginated. Males have a carapace length of up to 300mm, although they are actually around the same size as females - some of this extra length is due to the caudal marginal flaring. Females are usually

The same female Marginated Tortoise
(Testudo marginata).

around 220 to 280mm
carapace length. The
carapace itself is very dark
- often black with few
markings discernable.
The vertebral and costal
scutes may have lighter
coloured spots at their
centre and the marginals
which may bear black
triangles on a horn or
orangey background. There
is a single supracaudal scute.
Adult weight is between 2.0 and 3.0kgs. The
plastron bears pairs of triangular markings.
 A dwarf subspecies, *T. marginata
weissingeri* has been described from
Sardinia.

Temperament
Generally good, although
these are large tortoises
and so can do much
damage in a well
maintained garden. Males
however can be very
aggressive to other males
and females during breeding.

A large female Marginated
Tortoise *(Testudo marginata).*

Sex Difference
Males have an obvious narrower 'waist' than females and have a longer, thicker
tail. The marginals are more flared than in females.

Natural Habitat
Dry scrubby or rocky areas, even in to coastal areas.

Horsfield's or Russian Tortoise *Testudo (Agrionemys) horsfieldii*

Horsfield's or Russian Tortoise *Testudo (Agrionemys) horsfieldii* GRAY 1844 is a
species under a degree of taxonomic dispute as there are a few distinct
differences between this species and other Testudo species. These differences are
such that it has been recommended that Horsfield's tortoise be placed in its own

27

genus of Agrionemys. This question has not yet been resolved, and in the interests of simplicity I shall keep to the Testudo generic name in this book.

Description

The outline of the shell is roughly circular and this tortoise has a solid, stocky appearance. The colour of the carapace is a greenish-brown with poorly defined darker markings. It

A male Horsfield's or Russian Tortoise
Testudo (Agrionemys) horsfieldii

shares some features with Hermann's tortoise in that it has a spur-like scale on the tip of its tail (although this is not as prominent as with *T. hermanni*) and there is no hinge in the plastron. The skin on the legs, tail and neck is a brownish-yellow colour. There are only four toes on each foot, distinguishing it from other Testudo species which normally possess five toes on each of the front feet.

Horsfield's tortoise is principally an Asiatic species whose western range impinges upon the most eastern areas of the Mediterranean area. It is naturally found in Eastern Iran, Afghanistan, Kazakhstan, Pakistan (including Baluchistan). Its range extends from as far west as the Caspian Sea in the former USSR to western China in the east.

Size

These are not large tortoises. Maximum size is up to 200mm, with most usually significantly smaller.

Temperament

Male Horsfield's tortoises can be quite aggressive and can inflict serious bites on other tortoises. However they do not 'ram' quite so hard as seen in other Testudo species. Conversely this means that females should not be mixed with males of other species as they can be seriously damaged by this violent activity. They are excellent diggers and climbers. This species is very cold hardy but also requires an arid environment; damp, humid environments do predispose to respiratory disease. Finally the long hibernation periods of some populations of this tortoise - which can be up to nine months of the year - means that these tortoises are eating machines. As a result, obesity is a common problem in Horsfield's tortoises.

Sex Differences
Males have markedly longer tails. The plastron is usually flat in both sexes.
Females are larger.

Another view of the same male Horsfield's or
Russian Tortoise *Testudo (Agrionemys) horsfieldii*

Natural Habitat
This tortoise prefers open, grassy areas that are relatively dry so it is found on
sandy steppes, rocky ground or on hillsides. They dig burrows up to two metres
long with a widened chamber at the end; in Pakistan they are known to
appropriate the disused burrows of marmots. They can occur at high altitudes
and have been discovered at heights up to 2,300m above sea level.

29

EVOLUTION
AND
NATURAL HISTORY

Evolution (*208 Millions years ago to the present*)

Mediterranean tortoises belong to the order Testudines (or Chelonia). The evolution of this group can be documented reasonably well, albeit patchily, as far back as the Triassic Period (208 – 146 Million years ago (Myr)). Prior to this, the situation becomes unclear but a good starting point is to remember that tortoises are reptiles and so in order to attempt to chart their evolution, we need to consider where they fit within reptilian classification.

The Class Reptilia belongs to the Series Amniota. This includes all species that lay self-contained eggs, as well as their descendants. The amniotes are grouped as follows:

Anapsida. This includes many early forms as well as the tortoise lineages. Synapsida. This group contains the extinct mammal-like reptiles and the mammals.

Diapsida. The Diapsida includes the lizards, snakes, crocodilians, birds, dinosaurs and pterosaurs.

The first amniotes arose in the Mid-Carboniferous (310 –300 Myr) with early anapsids identifiable from the late Carboniferous and early Permian (290 Myr) periods. Based upon traditional systematics, the Anapsida not only contains the Testudines, but also Pareiasauridae and Procolophonidae. These other two families contained reptilian-like creatures that were generally large and either herbivorous or omnivorous. Along with the Millerettidae, these four families constitute a group known as the Parareptilia. More recent molecular studies, however, suggest that they may be more closely related to crocodilian lineages than previously thought.

Pareiasaurs and procolphonids of the Permo-Triassic are close relatives of the Testudines, to the extent of sharing a common ancestor. One fossil, Eunotosaurus, a procolophonid primitive reptile from the middle Permian (around 325 Myr) gives an indication of what may have happened in Testudine evolution. The neck on this species is long and there are ten dorsal vertebrae. The first eight of these are flattened and widened into leaf-like structures. The skin over these ribs carries a thin armour of bony scutes. The shoulder joints are overlapped by the first set of ribs, mimicking or possibly foreshadowing the arrangement seen in modern chelonia.

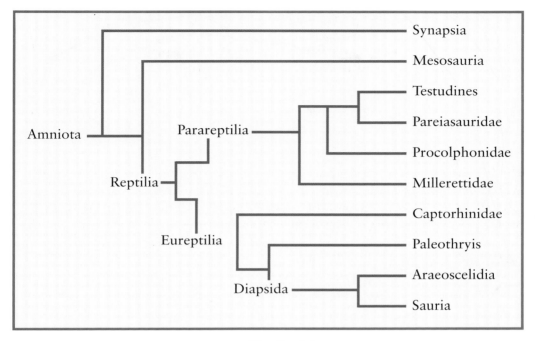

Fig. Evol 1

Triassic Period (250 to 208 Myr).

It is during this time period that we find the earliest examples of true chelonians such as Proganochelys from Germany, a sizable species with a shell up to two feet long. It was already land-living in habit and possessed a well developed shell with several large mid-line plates, lateral plates and smaller marginal plates that formed sharp projections around the rim of the shell. Unlike all other chelonians alive and extinct, it possessed teeth – not on the jaws but on the palate.

Jurassic Period (208 – 146 Myr)

Chelonians found at this time become identifiable as forming two major groups – the Pleurodira and the Cryptodira, which together form the clade Casichelydia. The main difference is that pleurodires pull their head in by making a sideways bend of the neck, whilst cryptodires curve their neck vertically. The ancestors of the Mediterranean species are obviously cryptodires and this group began a rapid radiation into six main clades during the late Jurrasic. Of these, three clades are now extinct - Kayentachelys, the baenids and meiolanids - and three are still present - the chelonoids (marine turtles) trionychoids (soft-shell turtles) and testudinoids (tortoises and terrapins).

31

Cretaceous Period (146 - 65 Myr)

The end of the Cretaceous saw mass extinctions throughout many groups of animal and plant life – most notably that of the dinsosaurs. Whatever the cause, be it cataclysmic disaster, climatic change or any other theory put forward, chelonians were not exempt. Nineteen families were distinguishable before the end of the Cretaceous. Only fifteen remained afterwards, giving an extinction rate of 27%.

Eocene Epoch (56 - 35 Myr)

The time between the Cretaceous and the Eocene known as the Paleocene (65 – 56Myr), had been characterised by an overall warming of the globe. Possibly facilitated by world's warm climate, by the time the Eocene had arrived not only had true Testudo species evolved, but they had spread to relatively northern areas. From the early Eocene two Testudo species (*T. doduni* and *T. corroyi*) are reported from France, whilst *Testudo comptoni* has been described from equivalent deposits in England. However the Eocene saw an overall fall in temperatures, by the order of 12°C, by its end. This may explain why Testudo fossils are only found in these high latitiudes in the early Eocene. Upper Eocene deposits elsewhere have yielded other fossils Testudo species such as *T. ammon* from Egypt and *T. grandidieri* from Madagascar.

Pliocene (5 – 1.6Myr) and Pleistocene (1.6 – 0.01 Myr) Epochs.

We now jump to the late Pliocene and the following Pleistocene, periods which were characterised by rapid and marked climatic fluctuations. It would appear that in Africa, the early to mid Pliocene (5 –3 Myr) was moister than present, with greater forest and tree cover and less desert. North Africa in particular seems to have been much moister than present day, with semi-arid vegetation covering the modern Sahara. Tropical forest and moist savanna extended quite far north. It was in this environment that the Mediterranean tortoise species evolved. Those tortoises familiar to us are

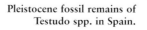

Pleistocene fossil remains of
Testudo spp. in Spain.

32

identifiable in the fossil record by the Pleistocene. The remains of the spur-thighed tortoise *T. graeca* are found throughout the Mediterranean area, whilst *T. hermanni* is found throughout its present range as well as Italy. Other Testudo remains extend into northern and eastern Europe including Russia and on into China, of which Horsfield's tortoise (*A. horsfieldii*) may well prove to be a remnant.

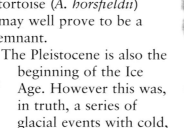

Carapacial details are obvious in these fossil remains of *Testudo spp.* in Spain

The Pleistocene is also the beginning of the Ice Age. However this was, in truth, a series of glacial events with cold, dry glacial periods interspersed with warmer and wetter times, often lasting only a few hundred to a couple of thousand years.

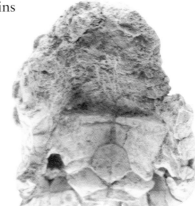

Plastron details are obvious in these fossil remains of *Testudo spp.* in Spain

Holocene Epoch (0.01Myr to present).

With the passing of the Ice Age we enter the Holocene and this too has been a rollercoaster – at least in North Africa where very wet and dry phases have alternated - some only lasting a few decades whilst others continuing for several centuries before ending abruptly. The gradual development and spread of the Sahara Desert separated the north African species from their central African cousins, allowing them to evolve along separate lines to those found south of that great desert.

However the above is to tell only part of the story. These tortoises have evolved over time, but they have become what they are by slowly changing as each species as a whole adapted to the local environmental pressures of the Mediterranean basin, which has itself had an eventful past.

Tectonic movements lead to the break up of the super-continent Pangea so that by the Triassic Period the Atlantic Ocean had formed between the North American plate and those of Africa and Eurasia. Crucially, other plate movements created a body of water between the African and Eurasian plates, known as the Tethys Ocean. This has existed from 340 Myr, but since the late Cretaceous this has been gradually narrowing as the African and Eurasian plates continued to converge. Its remains are the present Mediterranean Sea. During this time the Tethys Ocean has undergone progressive evaporation as it has shrunk, leaving high levels of calcium deposits in the underlying geology of its former range. The natural ranges of the Testudo species, with their high requirement for calcium, appear to be closely linked to those geographic areas originally covered by this sea.

The state of the Tethys Ocean itself has not been one of a progressive shrinkage. By the late Miocene Epoch, between five and six million years ago, the Tethys Ocean had become completely cut off from the Atlantic allowing a massive evaporation of its waters. This Messinian "salinity crisis" would have undoubtledly established land bridges that may well have allowed dispersal of Testudo ancestors across the region. Certainly there was an exchange of mammalian species between Spain and Morocco around this time.

In the Pliocene (5 – 2.4 Myr), a time when we know Testudo species were present, the Mediterranean basin became reconnected with the Atlantic, re-establishing the present ocean and as a result, cutting off the different tortoise populations into the areas we are familiar with today. This allowed subspeciation, and probably speciation, to occur in these widely separated groups. Without a doubt, the influence of this ancient ocean to Mediterranean tortoises cannot be overstated.

Throughout it all the terrestrial tortoises of the region have prevailed, no doubt in part to their evolved ability to push their physiology to extreme limits – such as hibernating or aestivating through prolonged periods of adverse climatic conditions. Now modern Mediterranean tortoises can be found in a variety of natural habitats, but there are certain common environmental factors present for all species.

Natural History - Sunlight

The Mediterranean is a very sunny area with an attendant holiday industry to prove it. It is 'sunny' because those countries around the Mediterranean receive, on average, 3,000 hours of sunlight a year. Unfortunately in Great Britian we receive only around 1,500 hours. Sunlight is probably the most fundamental environmental factor for tortoises. Not only does it provide light, but heat as well.

Looking at light further we can subdivide it into three important components:

Photoperiod – the length of the day and night vary seasonally over the year. During the peak summer there can be over 14 hours of daylight, whilst during the middle of winter daylength can be shortened to 10 to 12 hours. The tortoises monitor this with the pineal gland, and this helps to trigger the behavioural changes linked to preparation of hibernation, as well as feeding into the hormonal cycles linked to breeding.

Spectrum - This describes the wavelengths, or colours, of the incident light. Of particular interest is ultraviolet light. There are three groups of wavelength that are in the ultraviolet spectrum.

- Ultraviolet A (UVA) has wavelengths of 320 – 400 nm (nanometres). This appears to be important in triggering some normal behaviour patterns such as feeding. Tortoises can see in the ultraviolet spectrum and it may be that UVA affects how tortoises percieve their food and surroundings.
- Ultraviolet B (UVB) has wavelengths of 290 – 315 nm. It is this range of UV light that is important for vitamin D3 synthesis in the skin. Vitamin D3 is important not only in the uptake of dietary calcium, but is probably needed for normal skin and immune function.
- Ultraviolet C (UVC) has even shorter wavelengths – around 250 – 260 nm, and is the most dangerous type, linked with skin cancers and sunburn. Tortoises are well protected from UVC with their highly pigmented skins.
- Ultraviolet exposure is a variable factor in the wild and is influenced by cloud cover, vegetation cover, time of day and so forth. It is, however, of crucial importance to the wellfare of chelonia both in the wild and in captivity.

Intensity - Mid-summer sunshine in the Mediteranean is much more intense than that seen in more northerly lattitudes such as Great Britian. This is because at higher lattitudes, the slope of the earth means that there is a thicker layer of atmosphere for the sun's rays to penetrate through, and those rays are spread over a greater area than those closer to the equator.

Heat

As discussed in the first chapter, tortoises are ectotherms and rely primarily on the sun for warmth. Tortoises thermoregulate behaviourally so that, wherever possible, they maintain their body temperature at around 30°C by alternating their exposure to direct sunlight with that of shade. The high average hours of sunlight in the Mediterranean means that these tortoises can be active for substantial parts of the day, and for more days of the year than they could at more northerly lattitudes.

The main way that a tortoise controls its body temperature is by shuttling into and out of the sun, seeking shade when it starts to overheat. But this is a fairly crude means of doing so. Fine tuning can occur by altering the angle of the shell to increase or reduce the amount of shell directly exposed to the sun. This can be done by either turning the body at a right angle to the sun's rays so exposing as much of the surface area of the shell as possible, or turning towards or away from the sun to present a narrower area. Tilting the shell using the legs, or even selecting slopes or rocks to help them achieve just the right angle are common. Internally a tortoise is able to reduce or increase the blood flow to its skin and shell. If it wants to warm up rapidly it will increase the peripheral blood flow through the shell and skin to pick up as much heat as possible and transfer this to the rest of its organs and tissues. To slow down its rate of cooling, for example at night, it can shut down this superficial blood circulation to reduce its heat loss.

Shell colouring, particularly of the carapace, is also important. The colour black is the best absorber (and radiator) of heat. Those tortoise species found in more northerly areas such as Herman's tortoise, or at altitude such as Horsfield's tortoise, are darker than those from the more southerly countries. Even within *Testudo hermanni* populations those found at altititude are often darker. Many species found in very hot, sunny areas, such as the Libyan Spur-thighed tortoise, have a large amount of yellow in the carapace, reducing its heat absorbtive capacity and increasing its ability to reflect heat away.

Moisture

Mediterranean species are creatures of semi-arid to arid environments, with at best only seasonal rainfall. Many are found at relatively high altitidues, in particular Horsfield's tortoise being found at altitudes of up to 2,300m, which again places them in low moisture environments. High humidity can predispose them to respiratory problems, a situation complicated by their unique anatomy that means that they cannot cough efficiently to eradicate any build up of phlegm or mucus from their windpipe and lungs.

Vegetation

Vegetation plays an important part in the ecology of these tortoises. As inhabitants of semi-arid areas and drier forested regions, plants not only serve as food but they also provide cover from predators, act as territorial markers and help to create shady, humid retreats. For *Testudo kleinmanni*, certain grasses stabilize the sand dunes helping to create the structure of their habitat, whilst for *T. g. graeca*, clumps of the succulent Euphorbia provide permanent outcrops of shade in an environment that is only seasonally rich in vegetation. A key factor in most of the natural habitats of the Mediterranean tortoises is that the vegetation is largely undisturbed. Thus they are found on hillsides, woodland verges and well-established olive groves as well as more open, sandy and rocky places. At one extreme there is Herman's tortoise with a preference for significant levels of ground cover to *Testudo kleinmanni* which makes its home amongst the scrubby sand dunes of Egypt.

Typical habitat for Western Hermann's Tortoise
T. hermanni hermanni in Tuscany.
One is just visable in the centre of the photograph

Microclimates

In the relatively dry world that these tortoises have evolved in, microclimates assume a great importance. These are small, localised areas where the surrounding geography and vegetation impart an environment significantly different to that of the more generalized landscape. As an example, disused rodent burrows may offer both a relatively humid and cool environment in an otherwise baking landscape. In particular microclimates are utilized by hatchling and young tortoises. Here, under plants and rocks, these small and susceptible chelonia can hide from predators in environments that buffer them from the more severe challenges of life such as dehydration. The behaviour of such small tortoises is often very different from that of adults largely due to their more secretive ways.

Predation

Mediterranean tortoises occupy a similar ecological niche to small or medium-sized rodent and rodent-like herbivores such as rabbits. They convert energy assimilated by plants from the sun's rays into animal protein, but despite their protective armour-plating, like other herbivores they are still susceptible to predation. Adults are taken by large raptors such as bearded vultures and golden eagles, which will carry small to medium specimens as high as 30 metres before dropping them in an attempt to split open the shell. Several attempts may be needed. Pairs with chicks can potentially account for large numbers in the course of a breeding season. Ground predators such as wild boar, rats and foxes can prove to be significant plunderers of nests and hatchlings.

Tortoises and Man

Tortoise are popular as pets, as much for their behaviour as their appearance

A major cause of declining tortoise populations in the wild is man. Increasing urbanisation and 'improved' farming methods all encroach on natural tortoise habitat and eventually make it unsuitable for maintaining wild populations. Road traffic can also be a cause of significant mortalities.

In the past collection for the pet trade has been a serious cause of declining numbers of tortoises in the wild. Most of the

Mediterranean tortoises with the exception of Horsfield's tortoise are now covered by CITES legislation (*see Legislation*) although there is still a significant degree of illegal collection and sale in their native lands.

Behaviour

Part of the joy of keeping Mediterranean tortoises is their behaviour. Arguably not as intelligent as many bird and mammalian pets, for reptiles they are intelligent and will certainly learn to recognise their owner, just as their owner will learn that each tortoise is an individual with distinct likes, dislikes and behaviour patterns. In one study tortoise hatchlings (*Testudo graeca* and *T. hermanni*) were shown to not only to differentiate between colours but could also distinguish between different shaped objects (Fenwick 1995).

Tortoises are often said to be territorial. To some extent this is true, although it is probably more accurate to say that tortoises occupy a home range which is defended as occasion demands. The home range will encompass all that the tortoise needs to survive and the longer the tortoise remains there, the better it will come to know its home and so utilise it more effectively. The best basking spots for a given time of day will be remembered, as will the position of food and freestanding water, even though these may change according to the seasons. Favoured burrows or resting sites will be returned to time and again; the same place will often be selected for hibernation every year.

However the natural habitat of the tortoise is a nutritionally poor, harsh environment and its meagre resources will usually not sustain large numbers of individuals. In the wild densities of around one individual per 150 square metres are not uncommon, and depending upon the species and size of the individual they may be even more sparse. Over many years incumbent tortoises will spend a significant amount of time and effort on learning, by trial and error, how best to use their territory. With such a huge investment at stake, such home ranges need to be defended.

Male tortoises in particular are frequently territorial to a surprising degree, and will especially target other males. *Testudo ibera* males can be particularly aggressive and will cause serious damage to other, less aggressive species if housed together. They will bite and ram their opponent in an attempt to drive it out of their territory. In some cases they may even mount the other tortoise as a sign of dominance. Damage is commonly

Shell rot and underlying bone infection in a male *T. graeca* following damage from a male *T. g. ibera*.

sustained to the shell of the subordinate, particularly at the back end of the carapace, with loss of part of the keratin scutes and exposure of the underlying bone. Bites around the head and legs can also be seen. In some males this instinct is so strong that it can be shown against non-tortoise objects such as shoes and stones. Attempts to mate with these inanimate objects may also occur.

Red foot tortoises thinking about mating!.

Female tortoises will occasionally show similar behaviour, although it is rarely as intense as that seen in males. Signs of such territorial defence can be seen as early as one year old, although sexual maturity is normally not until around five years.

Separate from, but superficially similar in appearance to, territorial defence is mating behaviour. This can appear quite aggressive with males trailing and biting at exposed parts of the female. This is normal and is probably a significant stimulus, triggering ovulation to occur. In an enclosed space however, serious damage can occur if the female cannot escape the male's attentions. Often the first indication of mating behaviour is the clacking sound of shell against shell as the male bashes the front of his carapace against that of the female – a sure sign of attempted courtship. If pairs are watched it will then be seen that the male's actions are designed to stop the female from escaping, rather than actively repulse her. When receptive, the female may raise her back end to aid mating. The male will mount her (in some species this is aided by the concavity of the male's plastron, allowing him to fit better on the back of the female's carapace) and may vocalise during mating.

Inappropriate territorial and mating behaviour is common in captive collections where population densities are abnormally high. This can be exacerbated by incorrect sex ratios, for example there may be too many males, or inappropriate species mixes. In this situation both dominant and subordinate individuals can suffer. Subordinate tortoises may be prevented from accessing basking spots and gaining adequate food, which over a period of time will weaken them. Failure to reach their PBT because they cannot bask correctly will reduce their immunity as well as their ability to digest food and so on. Dominant tortoises may spend so much time attempting to drive out competitors, or repeat mating with females who cannot escape, that they too will have a reduced food intake and fatigue.

In general tortoises are relatively quiet animals. Many will hiss with disapproval if picked up, a sound made by a rapid expulsion of air as head and limbs are suddenly and forcefully drawn back into the shell. Male tortoises may vocalise during mating. In particular the Egyptain tortoise (*Testudo kleinmanni*) male makes a characterisitc bird-like oscillating call during copulation.

Fenwick, H 1995 Conservation –in a cold climate. Proceedings of International Congress of Chelonian Conservation, July 1995

Chapter Four

NUTRITION, DIET
AND
FEEDING

Water

The Mediterranean regions inhabited by tortoises are relatively dry environments. Like all animals, they have a need for water, yet they are unable to cover long distances like large mammals, or fly over natural obstacles as can birds, to reach a water-source. Tortoises have solved this problem by a combination of behavioural and internal means. Combined together these adaptations mean that Mediterranean tortoises are good at collecting water and keeping it for as long as possible.

Make no mistake about it, if a thirsty tortoise finds a river, a stream or a puddle of water after a rain storm, it will drink and pet tortoises should always have access to water. Tortoises do not have a soft palate at the back of their mouth as we have that allows them to separate the back of the mouth from the nasal chambers. This means that whilst drinking, a tortoise will often submerge its nostrils underneath the surface of the water to stop sucking in air as it swallows.

If there is no access to free water then the tortoise's main sources are from its food or from its own internal metabolic reactions. Green leafy material, in particular the softer buds of plants, have a high moisture content and are a valuable resource, especially if the tortoise is able to feed early in the day when vegetation may have a covering of dew. Dandelion leaves, for example, contain around 86% water whereas commercially produced foods – produced to be as

Tortoises should be given access to water

succulent as possible for the human palate – will have higher water contents e.g. Romaine lettuce (94% water).

Many of the natural chemical reactions that occur inside the body generate molecules of water as part of their end product. Even though these metabolic reactions are at the level of individual cells, the water produced can be a significant percentage of the tortoise's total water needs.

The urinary bladder acts as the most important water store in terrestrial chelonia. When full, it can occupy up to 40% of the volume inside the shell. Urine produced by the kidneys is transported down small tubes known as ureters into the bladder, where it is stored. If the tortoise is in danger of becoming dehydrated it can absorb water directly across the lining of the bladder and back into its body – a feat that we mere mammals are unable to do.

Water is lost from the body in four main ways:

Evaporation from the skin. Tortoises have a very thick skin through which very little water can evaporate. They also do not have sweat glands and will usually keep cool by selecting an environment that is at a lower temperature. Seriously overheated tortoises may attempt to keep their heads cool by salivating so much that they appear to froth at the mouth, attempting to cool by allowing the saliva to evaporate. This behaviour is obviously very wasteful of water and is only used in dire circumstances.

As water vapour during breathing. Little is lost this way, but it is important because the tortoise can do little to prevent it as it comes from the moist lining of the lungs and trachea. This route of water loss becomes particularly crucial during hibernation.

In urine. As described earlier, tortoise kidneys, like those of other reptiles, are unable to concentrate their urine to reduce water loss. This is why they further reabsorb urinary water from the cloaca, large intestine, and bladder and eliminate much of their waste nitrogen as uric acid.

In faeces. This is probably the route by which most water is lost from the body. Inappropriate diets and gut infections can contribute to this water loss considerably.

Tortoises will seek out relatively humid microclimates such as rodent burrows, dense thickets of vegetation and the like. These places are not in the sun and so do not dry out quickly. Plants transpire, releasing minute amounts of water vapour from their leaves into their immediate environment making the local humidity higher than in the open. Such relatively humid air may reduce the rate of water loss particularly from the lungs.

All captive tortoises should have access to clean water supplied in an easily accessable container. If this cannot be supplied then the tortoise should be placed in a shallow bath at least every other day for around thirty minutes to allow it to drink. As a guide the water level of the bath should be at the junction of the carapace and the plastron.

Food and Feeding

General Principles of Tortoise Nutrition

There is much misinformation about the feeding of Mediterranean tortoises in the literature. Refer back to the notes on their specialised digestive anatomy. These animals are vegetarians and so a good place to start is look at their preferred foods. The table below compares the contribution of the major food types to the energy needs of the three main feeding groups of reptiles.

Dietary Energy Content	Carnivore	Omnivore	Herbivore
Protein	25-60	15-40	15-35
Fat	30-60	5-40	less than 10
Carbohydrate	less than 10	20-75	55-75

(Taken from Donoghue S. 1995 Clinical Nutrition of Reptiles and Amphibians in Proceedings Association of Reptilian and Amphibian Veterinarians)

So Mediterranean tortoises, as herbivores, obtain most of their energy (55-75%) from carbohydrates, with less from protein (15-35%) and little (less than 10%) from fats. Now lets look at their natural diet. For the wild Spur-thighed tortoise (*T. graeca*), its diet consists mostly of the Plantain family Plantago (30%), the Daisy family Compositae (26%)and Bedstraw family Rubiaceae (10%). For *Testudo hermanii* diet largely constituted consisted of Bedstraw family (25%), Peaflower family Leguminosae (22%), Daisy family (10%) and Buttercup family Ranunculaceae (8%) (Swingland 1984). Of particular note is that this diet gives an average calcium to phosphorus ratio of 3.5:1 and a typical protein content of 2.75%.

Some species specific guidelines have been suggested by Highfield (2000). These are:

• Spur-thighed tortoises (*Testudo graeca* and *T. ibera*): Mixed flowers, succulent plants and green leaves. Fruit and carbohydrate rich diets are problematic.
• Hermann's tortoise (*Testudo hermanni*): Mixed flowers and green leaf material.
• Egyptian tortoise (*Testudo kleinmanni*): Mixed flowers, succulent plants and green leaves. Fruit is problematic.

• Russian tortoise (*Testudo horsfieldi*): Mixed flowers and green leaves. Avoid fruit.

Referring back to the wild-type diet, if we consider that the parts of the plant that are usually eaten are the leaves and flowers, then we can come up with a simple mantra for the type of food that Mediterranean tortoises ought to be given. Their diet should be:

High in fibre: Offering green and leafy foods as the mainstay of their diet is a good way of ensuring plenty of fibre. Ideal foods would include dandelion leaves (and flowers), grasses, sow thistle, clover and watercress. Despite their bad press, various lettuces are useful as part of the food intake. They are a good source of water and are usually so palatable to the tortoise that they will accept it even when coated with vitamin and mineral supplements.

High in calcium: Tortoises have a high requirement for calcium, and work with wild North American gopher tortoises (*Gopherus agassizi*) has demonstrated that they will selectively seek out and eat those plants with naturally high calcium levels (Highfield 2000). It is highly probable that Mediterranean species do so as well. The availability of calcium to the animal is governed by a number of different factors, one of which is the level of phosphorus present. Phosphorus, in the form of phosphate, combines with calcium to form complexes that render calcium unavailable to the tortoise. So the more phosphate that is present the less calcium is accessible. Most animals appear to need on average a calcium to phosphorus ratio of 2:1. As detailed above for *Testudo graeca*, 3.5:1 appears to be more appropriate.

Low in protein: Protein levels should be kept low. Mediterranean tortoises are almost exclusively vegetarian, but their wild-diet is so nutritionally poor that should they come across the carcass of a bird or similar, they will eat it as a means of enhancing their protein intake. This is a survival instinct that allows tortoises in the wild to maximize their use of the environment. This is different from regularly feeding them on dog or cat food on a regular basis, a practice which only spells disaster long term. Unfortunately the high protein levels of these foods do make them tasty to the tortoise but the urge to feed them on these should be resisted. Protein is used for growth and energy, but an excessive intake not only leads to abnormally high growth rates (see Excessive Protein Intake) but also to fatty liver and kidney disease as excess energy is converted into fat and stored in these, and other organs.

Food	Protein %	Fat %	Carbohydrate %
Fruits	1-10	0-5	85-95
Vegetables	5-30	0-10	60-95
Greens	15-40	0-10	50-85
Tinned Dog Food	20-30	15-40	30-65
Tinned Cat Food	30-45	30-45	10-40

Taken from (Taken from Donoghue S. 1995 Nutrition Support in Proceedings Association of Reptilian and Amphibian Veterinarians)
Comparing the energy profile of tinned dog and cat foods we can see that they are completely unsuitable for feeding Mediterranean tortoises on. Interestingly enough the same can be said of fruits and certainly no more than 10% of their diet should be fruit-based.

Nutrient Content of Food

Food consists of a variety of different nutritional elements that need to be considered. These add up to the quality of any given food. Good quality food provides what the tortoise requires whilst poor quality food is either deficient in some or all of these aspects, or else is inappropriate for the needs of the tortoise.

Water is an essential part of the nutritional content of food as we have seen. In addition to feeding the correct foods, clean, free-standing water should always be available.

Protein: is needed for growth and repair of the body. Mediterranean tortoises are adapted to a low protein diet, but by feeding standard "supermarket" foods it is very easy to overdo this leading to gut disorders and problems with excessive growth.

Fat: is utilized relatively poorly by these tortoises. Some fat is needed however, especially by reproductively active females as most of the egg yolk consists of fatty materials which are an ideal store of energy for the developing embryo. Because of this, the types of fat consumed by female tortoises may affect the viability of any eggs produced by her. Too high a fat diet can result in hepatic lipidosis.

Carbohydrates: are the main energy source for terrestrial chelonia. Primarily these are the simple sugars and starches produced by plants during photosynthesis. These carbohydrates are absorbed in the small intestine. Excessive carbohydrate intake can not only lead to gut upsets, but also hepatic lipidosis as excess is converted into fat and stored in the liver.

Fibre: is important in two main ways. First of all part of it is digested by gut bacteria which break it down to smaller molecules that can be absorbed and used by the tortoise. Secondly its presence promotes normal gut motility and stool formation, both of which are vital to a normal gut environment.

Vitamins: Just like with us, tortoises require a number of vitamins to remain healthy. Vitamins can broadly be divided into water-soluble and fat-soluble. The water soluble vitamins cannot generally be stored and so need to be manufactured and used as needed. Fat soluble vitamins on the other hand can be stored in the body's fat reserves.

Water Soluble Vitamins:
• The B vitamins are largely produced by the gut bacteria and are absorbed

directly across the gut wall. This means that deficiencies are rare in Mediterranean tortoises, although they can occur in cases of extreme anorexia or prolonged antibiotic use.
• There is no evidence for a dietary requirement for vitamin C in tortoises.
Fat Soluble Vitamins:
• Vitamin D_3 is required to absorb calcium out of the gut and into the body. Without it calcium cannot be absorbed in significant quantities, even if a large amount is present in the food. It is produced in several stages. First of all previtamin D is converted to a second compound – previtamin D – in the skin under the presence of ultraviolet light. Previtamin D is then further converted to vitamin D_3 by a second reaction, but this is a temperature dependant change and so the tortoise must be at its preferred body temperature for this to happen. Vitamin D_3 is then further converted into more active substances in both the liver and kidneys.

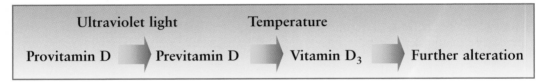

Vitamin D_3 is of animal origin and when supplied as a dietary supplement is considered to be the only form that tortoises and other reptiles can utilise. This is important as many pet shop vitamin supplements contain vitamin D_2 which is plant derived (and therefore cheaper) but will be of no use to the tortoise.
• Vitamin E, often in conjunction with selenium, is needed for normal muscle and reproductive function. It also helps to prevent stored fats turning rancid (steatitis).
• Vitamin A is important for the normal integrity and functioning of body linings especially the lining of the respiratory tract. Deficiencies in vitamin A causes changes in these linings leaving the tortoise more susceptible to secondary respiratory infections, even pneumonia. Also affected are the tearglands in the eyelids and the microscopic tubules in the kidneys, causing eye and kidney disease. Coloured (red, orange and yellow) vegetables are a good source of vitamin A.
Minerals: The mineral content of food is largely a reflection of the underlying geology. For Mediterranean tortoises the most important mineral in the diet that we need to consider is calcium, doubly so because many of the foods offered to tortoises are low in this substance. As we have seen it is needed in large quantities compared to other minerals. Magnesium and phosphorus are also needed in reasonable quantities but are often present in high levels in most plant material. Fortunately most of the other necessary minerals, including trace elements, will be supplied by feeding a wide variety of appropriate foods, plus giving the tortoises access to soil.

Practical Feeding

Leafy greens such as dandelion leaves, watercress, nasturtiums, lettuces, sow thistle and clover should be the mainstay for the diet of these tortoises. Watercress and dandelion leaves – both naturally high in calcium, are particularly recommended. Many supermarkets offer bags of pre-washed salad greens that can be utilized as a core diet, but better still would be homegrown organic greens, especially as the nutritional characteristics of these foods could be enhanced by attention to the soil that they are grown

Dandelion leaves are a favourite food
for Mediterranean tortoises

in. As an example the calcium content of lettuce could possibly be increased by adding this mineral to the soil that it's grown in. These greens are often well accepted even when coated with mineral supplements.

Some greens should only be given in moderation. Members of the cabbage family such as cauliflowers, brussel sprouts and broccoli should be offered as no more than 10% of the total diet as they contain substances called goitrogens that antagonise thyroxine and so can induce low thyroxine levels (hypothyroidism). Spinach, rhubarb leaves and daffodils contain oxalic acid, which can be irritant to the gut lining or can trigger bladder stone formation as well as binding calcium into a form that is unavailable to the tortoise.

Flowers: as well, including dandelions and nasturtiums are readily taken. Be careful when offering flowers however, as some may be toxic. Deaths have been recorded from feeding just a few daffodil flowers.

Vegetables: are also useful as adjuncts to leafy greens. Cucumbers and courgettes are valuable sources of water. Red and yellow vegetables such as peppers and grated carrots can be offered. If eaten they provide a good source of vitamin A. Tomatoes are frequently offered and although they too are a good source of water, nutritionally they are acceptable only as a small percentage of the tortoise's diet.

Beans and peas: These are relatively high in protein and are often readily taken – on occasion to the exclusion of other foods. The protein content can be too high in these foods, and they also contain phytic acid that, like oxalic acid, will bind calcium into a form unavailable to the tortoise.

47

A female Turkish spur thighed tortoise enjoying the (occasional!) stawberry

Fruits: As mentioned earlier, the dietary profile of fruits is inappropriate in general for these animals. In the wild Mediterranean tortoises will feed on fallen or discarded fruit as a means of supplementing their diet. This is different from being fed fruit on a daily basis. Banana in particular can be a problem. It is readily taken by most tortoises but if fed in excess, the high carbohydrate levels can lead to gut upsets. It has also been tentatively linked with ear abscesses. Feed no more than 10% fruit.

Meat in any form: especially tinned dog or cat food, should never be given to captive Mediterranean tortoises. The protein and fat levels are far too high, and the level of vitamin supplements given in these foods is also so high that vitamin overdose becomes a real possibility. It is unfortunate that to many tortoises this type of food is very palatable and in nature they will occasionally feed on the carcasses of dead birds and so on. This is not surprising as their wild-type diet is low in protein, and so the opportunity to scavenge a ready source of protein would not be overlooked. As with fruits, this is an altogether different situation from daily feeding – a practice that will eventually lead to severe liver and kidney disease. As another example it is often said that tortoises will take snails. My own experience is that a healthy tortoise will usually ignore these gastropods.

Dietary Supplements: If in doubt it is better to err on the side of caution and provide a vitamin /mineral supplement than not to. Calcium is best supplied in a commercial calcium supplement, of which there are many available on the market. Many of these are combined with multivitamin complexes. If you opt for these do make sure that it is a supplement designed with reptiles in mind and so has vitamin D3, not vitamin D2. If there is good provision of ultraviolet light, either from natural sunlight or from full spectrum lighting, then calcium carbonate, or even limestone, can be given. Wherever possible make sure that the calcium supplement is phosphorus free. Egg shells, although consisting largely of calcium carbonate, do need sterilising first to reduce the risk of Salmonella infections.

Pelleted foods: There are now some very good pelleted foods available for tortoises, although some brands are far too high in protein for herbivorous species. They are usually very palatable and form a good basis for a tortoise's diet as they contain good levels of calcium and vitamins. The fibre levels of most pelleted foods are also often too low – an ideal would be 18 to 20% but this can affect the binding of the pellets and so it is often lower than this. Overall fibre levels can be increased by adding leafy greens to the pellet mixture. Pelleted foods should not be used exclusively, but can be useful in emergencies where fresh food is not readily available.

Feeding: Tortoises are grazers. They bite off choice pieces of plant material and then move on. Rarely will they stay in one place and graze a plant until it is level with the ground. The practical result of this is that if a tortoise is presented with a pile of food, it will eat some and is then likely to walk through the remaining food, possibly spoiling it further by defaecating or urinating on it. This may appear wasteful and frustrating for the tortoise owner but is perfectly natural behaviour. Therefore, where possible, food should be offered in relatively small amounts twice daily, to reduce waste and mimic a more natural feeding pattern.

For tortoises kept at large in the garden, often allowing them to graze on the lawn and in the herbaceous borders with only a minimum of dietary supplementation is often best. This will closely mimic their wild-type diet. A good sign is if the faeces are well formed, dark and fibrous. Runny faeces, considered by many to be normal, can be a sign of parasitism but is more likely to be the result of too low a fibre intake.

Normal tortoise faeces should be dark, firm and
fibrous, not loose and mucousy

Diet Related Diseases

Diseases and problems related to improper diet are quite common in Mediterranean tortoises. The anatomy of the digestive system has already been described.

Anorexia

Anorexia, or loss of appetite, is not a disease in itself but can be a sign of ill health. Tortoises not kept at their Preferred Body Temperature (PBT) may simply not eat. In cold weather outdoor tortoises may literally 'shut down' until warmer weather returns. This is normal and should not be a cause of concern.

Some male tortoises, especially the smaller North African *Testudo graeca's* that have been kept individually for years, will develop a relative anorexia at the same time as developing hypersexual behviour, with increased aggression or sexual attention being heaped upon inanimate objects such as shoes and rocks. This often occurs early in the year and can begin as soon as they come out of hibernation. Such males may need a hormone injection to settle them back to a more normal behavioural pattern.

If temperature and everything else appears ideal then veterinary attention should be sought to begin to investigate other possible causes such as infection, egg binding and so on.

Loose Faeces

This is common in tortoises fed on a high plane of nutrition, particularly a high fruit/low fibre diet. Here large amounts of soluble sugars and starch are not digested but passed further along the bowel than they should. Bacteria present in the gut ferment these into lactic acid. This can itself trigger diarrhoea but it also will cause a fall in the pH of the gut. This will kill off many of the beneficial bacteria naturally found there, further upsetting the digestive system. High levels of fat and protein in the bowel affect bacterial fermentation of the gut contents, and can produce foul smelling and greasy faeces as they are degraded by bacteria.

Excessive Protein Intake

This is seen in young, rapidly growing tortoises fed on a diet where their protein intake is too high relative to their calcium intake. Those structures made of proteins develop abundantly. In particular this applies to the keratin scutes, cutting edges of the mouth and claws. The bones of the skeleton have both a protein and mineral component, and so suffer doubly. The low calcium and high protein intake mean that the skeleton develops abnormally. The bones of the shell are not mineralised properly making them weak and easily deformed; the limb bones become over long but are weak and tend to bend and deform under the weight of the tortoise. Affected tortoises often show the following deformities:

The scutes of the shell are of a grossly mounded appearance as excessive keratin is produced. Because the underlying bony skeleton is not growing there is nowhere for the newly formed keratin to go but up! The scutes also have a "plastic" like appearance, quite unlike that of normal, healthy tortoises.

The shell is soft, because calcium is being continually drawn out of the bone and into the blood stream where it is used for normal muscle function and other physiological activities. Only once 60 to 70% of the calcium has been withdrawn from the shell will it appear soft so by the time this can be felt, the tortoise is already well on the road to severe problems. Affected tortoises have shells that can be easily compressed (remember if you do this it is probably painful to the tortoise) and the carapace often slopes from front to back because the front part is supported by the regular withdrawal of the head and neck.

The most plastic-looking appearance of the shell of this young *T. hermanii* suggests a problem with diet.

These tortoises often have difficulty walking because the long bones of the limbs and the joints themselves, especially the knee joints, are deformed. Some tortoises are physically unable to lift themselves up.

The beaks of these tortoises are often grossly overgrown – partly because too much keratin is produced and partly because these reptiles are often on too soft a diet such as lettuce leaves only.
Claws are often overgrown, partly due to keratin overproduction and partly because these tortoises are unable to walk properly and so their claws are not worn down.

In those tortoises with extremely low blood calcium levels they may go very floppy. This is because all muscles (including the heart muscle) need calcium to function correctly. Tortoises this badly affected carry a very poor outlook.

Note that by one year old the carapace and plastron should be solid in

This young *T. graeca* suffers from an excessive protein intake realative to calcium. The carapace is flattened and slopes from front to back. The shell was palapably soft.

The shell of this *T. hermanii* was so soft that when chewed by a family dog, the shell was easily puntured

a healthy tortoise. Young tortoises in the wild will take around ten years to reach a carapace length of 10cm. In captivity I have seen captive bred tortoises reaching adult size at eighteen months old, accompanied by gross skeletal deformities. Always aim for a slower growth rate by selecting an appropriate diet.

The above picture also largely describes a classic calcium deficient tortoise, or one that has been deprived of ultraviolet light or vitamin D3. The causes are subtly different but the result is the same. All of these conditions are often described together under the term Metabolic Bone Disease.

Metabolic Bone Disease

Bone diseases can be common in chelonia of all species, and any limb swelling, fracture or paralysis should be considered as a possible sign of an underlying bone disorder. Metabolic Bone Disease is actually a group of skeletal disorders that are largely – but not exclusively - dietary related. Common causes include a dietary calcium deficiency, a dietary calcium/phosphorus imbalance, a dietary vitamin D3 deficiency, lack of exposure to ultra violet light, dietary protein deficiency or excess and liver, kidney or intestinal disease.

However most skeletal problems are dietary linked, the clinical manifestations of which are often very similar and follow those listed under Excessive Protein Intake. Should a tortoise start to manifest such signs then one should immediately consider the following:

Diet: Reassess the possible protein, fibre and mineral content of the diet. Consider increasing or improving the calcium content of the diet.

Lighting: Make sure there is provision for ultraviolet lighting. There are some very good full spectrum fluorescent tubes available now, plus the newer lights that emit both ultraviolet and radiant heat. If fluorescent tubes are used check that their positioning is appropriate (usually around 30cm above the animal) close to a heat source(to encourage basking) and that they are changed regularly (every eight to twelve months). Supplementing with dietary or injectable vitamin D3 may be worth considering, but overdose can occasionally occur.

Temperature: Encourage a temperature drop at night if the tortoise seems otherwise well.

If the tortoise shows severe signs or is lethargic or anorexic then seek veterinary advice as secondary infections are common in such animals. Your tortoise may need radiographs, blood tests or other tests to establish what is causing the problem. Treatments can include injecting vitamin D3, injecting calcium plus dealing with other underlying causes such as liver disease.

Hepatic Lipidosis

Also referred to as fatty liver, this is a poorly understood condition where huge quantities of fat are laid down in the liver to an extent where it can affect the functioning of this vital organ. Such tortoises are often very heavy and have little or non-existent appetites. Females are more frequently affected and a Pre-Ovulatory Ovarian Stasis (see Reproduction Related Disorders) often occurs concurrently. Thyroid levels are often low. The immunity of the tortoise is compromised and so secondary infections are common. Treatment involves thyroid supplementation and occasionally anabolic steroids in an attempt to stimulate metabolism to burn off the stored fat. It may take many months to effect a cure.

Hypovitaminosis A

A lack of vitamin A is occasionally encountered, although I find it commoner in young red-eared sliders (*Trachemys scripta elegans*) than I do in Mediterranean tortoises. Affected individuals show a variety of eye problems such as swollen eyelids and a whitish accumulation may develop behind the lower lid. Changes in the tiny renal tubules can also occur, causing kidney damage. Affected chelonia are often anorexic as they cannot see to locate food. Treatment is with vitamin A supplementation. This can be given by injection by your veterinary surgeon to start with and then continued as a dietary supplement.

References
Highfield A.C. 2000 The Tortoise and Turtle Feeding Manual, Carapace Press UK

Swingland (1984) Dietary Preferences of Free Living Chelonians. Symposium on Chelonian Nutrition and Malnutrition, University of Bristol.

Chapter Five

Housing

The complexity or simplicity of housing necessary for the correct keeping of Mediterranean tortoises depends very much upon the species and life-stage of the tortoises that one is keeping. The simplest way is keeping hardy chelonia such as Herman's tortoise (*Testudo hermanni*) and *Testudo ibera* free range in a walled garden or large, naturalised pen. Other species such as *Testudo kleinmanni* and *Testudo nabulensis*, require vivaria or 'tortoise tables' for them

to thrive long-term. This also applies to hatchling and young members of the other species as well. However each method of care is not exclusive to the others and can be mixed, for instance keeping the more delicate species in runs outside in the summer often works to their benefit, whilst sick adults of the hardier species can be overwintered in vivaria.

Hardy tortoises such as *T. ibera* can be kept free-range in the garden

Many people have only one tortoise – often a family heirloom passed down from one generation to the next. Tortoises are not generally sociable and are relatively territorial so this will cause the individual no hardship. However once word gets out that you have a tortoise, it is not uncommon for other tortoises to come your way, often as unwanted gifts from people who have inherited them. In this way one can inadvertently begin to build up quite a motley collection of chelonia. So before we look at the types of accommodation that can be provided for tortoises whether you have one or many, here are some general recommendations on keeping groups of tortoises together:

Never mix species. This is for both behavioral and veterinary reasons. The first is that some species such as *Testudo ibera* are generally more aggressive than others. This applies particularly to males who will violently attack other males. Again, circumstantially at least, it appears that *T. ibera* may be a carrier for a cause of Runny Nose Syndrome. Large collections of North African *T. graeca* have been decimated following the introduction of an apparently healthy (Turkish origin) *T. ibera*.

Wherever possible only keep one male to a pen. In larger pens or gardens where there is plenty of room for escape and avoidance evenly matched males may occasionally develop a kind of truce, but this cannot be relied upon. Females can, in general, be kept in groups without there being too much aggression.

In mixed sex groups, a minimum ratio of 1:2 males to females is recommended, with preferably even more females. This spreads out the arduous attentions of the male over more females. Never keep more males than females.

Vivaria

Vivaria are enclosed, often rectangular indoor housings. The most difficult aspect of keeping tortoises and other reptiles in vivaria is how to recreate the sun in the box. The sun provides tortoises with both light and heat and as we have seen in Natural History, is crucial to these animals. In the majority of cases reptile keepers find it most convenient to separate lighting from heating and this is reflected in the commercially available products. This separation of these two key elements allows independent control where necessary.

Heat. In its simplest form this can be provided by a spotlight or other tungsten bulb. It is a radiant heat source like the sun and it will encourage tortoises to bask beneath it. Ideally it should be placed at one end of the vivarium so that a temperature gradient forms, allowing the tortoise to choose

Modern vivaria come in a variety of different materials and styles.

the temperature it prefers. These lights should be connected to a thermostat so that the vivarium does not overheat, and to a timer so that the light is not for 24 hours a day, or worse still is perpetually flicking on and off as the thermostat reacts to the temperature. To get around this there are ceramic bulbs available that only give out radiant heat and these are to be preferred. Such bulbs can provide radiant heat throughout the day and night irrespective of the lighting regime. Also red bulbs are available which produce heat and only visible red light, which is less disturbing to the tortoises at night. There are some blue bulbs available that emit light in the UVA spectrum. Heat mats are also readily available. These are placed either under the vivarium or on the side to provide localised warm areas; they are, however, insufficient to warm a whole vivarium and should be considered as supplementary heating only. They can help to produce warm microclimates under bark or similar that will be appreciated by hatchlings.

Always make sure your tortoise cannot directly touch the heat source as burns can occur.

Temperature beneath the basking light should be around 35°C with a background temperature of around 20 to 25 °C. A night time fall is to be recommended and temperatures down to 15 °C are easily tolerated, even by hatchlings.

Lighting is provided by full spectrum fluorescent tubing. Incident sunlight is not sufficient as glass filters out any UV lighting in particular, making it useless

Red footed tortoise basking under a heat lamp.

for tortoises. The fluorescent tubes available to herpetologists emit light in the most important parts of the spectrum including UVB and UVA. However light intensity falls off inversely with distance from that light source so that if one doubles the distance between the tortoise and the light tube, the intensity of the light is halved. This is important as suspending a full spectrum light several feet above a tortoise will be of little use. The ideal distance will usually be supplied by the manufacturer, but if in doubt suspend the tube around 30 to 45cm above the top of the carapace. Ideally the tubes should extend the full length of the vivarium, but if not situate them close to the heat source so that the tortoise will be exposed to the beneficial lighting as it basks. Because light intensity is important I would recommend using at least two such tubes to help imitate Mediterranean conditions. The lighting is best connected to a timer so that that the tortoise has a regular day: night pattern. I would suggest around 14 hours day to 10 hours night. This also gives us the ability to manipulate the lighting regime to help with preparation for breeding or hibernation if required. Be careful of how you select the fluorescent tubes. Always buy those specifically made for reptiles as many fluorescents said to mimic the sun are colour rendered to deceive our eyes and do not emit the correct spectrum. Glass filters out UV light and so these tubes are made from quartz – which makes them more expensive than ordinary fluorescents. Price therefore can be a rough guide to your purchase.

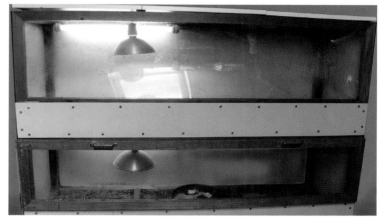

Unfortunately the UV output declines over time and these tubes do need replacing every eight to twelve months. This is a common cause of metabolic bone disease in tortoises kept in vivaria.

In the past few years lighting that emits both the correct spectrum and heat have become available and work well. Combining the two

Heat. In its simplest form this can be provided by a spotlight or other tungsten bulb

obviously better mimics natural sunlight but it does take away some of the flexibility inherent in having both functions separate.

Cleanliness becomes a serious issue with vivaria or in any relatively restricted enclosure. It is very tempting to try to set up naturalistic landscapes in vivaria and some do succeed well, but tortoises are inadvertently destructive creatures that will rapidly bulldoze through any habitat arrangements. Such vivaria are harder to maintain clean. Urine soaks readily into the substrate and faeces can be missed; there may even be a disincentive to remove soiled material in case in spoils the appearance of the vivarium. It is better all round to keep to a basic setup using newspaper as a substrate. This is cheap and cheerful and can be easily removed if soiled.

Modern vivaria come in a variety of different materials and styles. The simplest and least desirable are those based on an aquarium or fish tank. Although easy to find, their generally small size and poor ventilation make them unsuitable as anything but temporary housing. Along with the majority of reptiles, tortoises appear to have difficulty recognising the glass sides as a barrier and will spend hours clunking up and down the tank attempting to move on. Cleaning too is often difficult as access to the interior is from above. Proper reptile vivaria are much better for captive tortoises. They are made from many different substances including wood, MDF and plastics and can either be bought ready made, as flat packs or built yourself. To some extent their potential size and scope is limited only by the available space and the depth of your wallet. Key features for good vivaria are:

Access is via lockable sliding doors at the front of the vivarium. This greatly simplifies routine maintenance.

Water proofing. Tipped water containers and normal bladder functioning can lead to rotting wood unless the joints are silicone sealed. Use one designed for aquaria, not bathroom sealants that contain potentially toxic fungicides.

Ventilation is crucial to the well being of our tortoises. Normally ventilation is achieved by installing grids of mesh or plastic at opposite ends of the vivarium. Normally these grids are positioned at different heights so that as warm air rises it exits from the higher ventilation panel whilst fresh air is drawn in from the lower. There are also small fans available, which can either be connected to a timer, or better still to a thermostat so that they are switched on when the temperature in the vivarium becomes too high.

Tortoise Tables

These are a novel way of keeping tortoises indoors. They are based on a table structure where the table top is surrounded by a lip or wall of sufficient height to stop the tortoise from climbing out. Heating and lighting is as described under Vivaria, but is suspended over the table. The advantages of this housing are that the surface area available for the tortoises is much larger than is generally the case with vivaria; ventilation is excellent and it also brings the tortoises up to a level that allows you to interact with them more easily. Just make sure that there is no way that the tortoise can scale the walls!

Greenhouses and other Outdoor Buildings

Greenhouses and conservatories have the advantage of space and, with the correct choice of materials, exposure to natural heat and sunshine. Temperature

A spacious greenhouse with an outside run is ideal for summer accommodation

is often higher inside the greenhouse than out, but it can fluctuate wildly depending upon levels of sunshine. Shading of some description may be needed to iron out temperature instabilities (although this will inevitably reduce exposure to sunlight), or better still install automatic greenhouse vents that open and close as the temperature rises or falls.

The base of the

greenhouse should be solid - either brick or wooden –to present a solid boundary to the incumbent tortoises. Glass is inappropriate for the main panels and roof as it filters out 95% of the incident UVB, so it is better to replace it with special acrylics and Plexiglas which allow much higher percentages to pass through.

Thermostatically controlled heat lamps and full spectrum lighting can be suspended over the floor or individual pens to increase the hours of 'daylight' during the winter if necessary, and under soil heating can be used although there is a risk of entanglement if using soil warming cables with egg-laying or burrowing tortoises.

Other outbuildings such as sheds and garages can be pressed into use and with a combination of tortoise tables and stacking vivaria one can create an ideal setup for the care and raising of these tortoises.

The Garden

Large individuals of the hardier species including *Testudo hermanni, T. ibera, T. marginata* and *T. whitei* can be kept outdoors from the spring into late autumn. If the garden is not escape proof then large pens are necessary to provide plenty of natural grazing. Pens can also be utilized for smaller species such as Horsfield's tortoise (*T. horsfieldi*) and as summer accommodation for the other species. The advantages of keeping tortoises outdoors are:

1. Availability of space. Many of these tortoises are medium to large in size and require a lot of space to move around in.

2. Natural grazing. A more natural diet is easily provided by keeping tortoises on grass and clover and allowing them access to wild plants such as dandelions.

3. Exposure to unfiltered sunlight. We know how important sunlight is to these reptiles and so exposure to it can only be good (provided shelters are also available).

Female T. Ibera cropping grass.

4. Exposure to natural environmental cues. This includes seasonal variations in day length that trigger pre-hibernation behaviour.

There are some downsides however:

1. Exposure to potential predators. Rats, foxes, magpies and even pet dogs can predate, or at least badly injure, tortoises at liberty in the garden.

2. Exposure to 'natural' hazards. This would include a variety of dangers

including garden ponds (which should, wherever possible, be fenced off) and lawnmowers. Some garden plants may be toxic such as daffodils and foxgloves (*Digitalis sp*). Parasitic build up. In particular gardens can become contaminated with roundworm eggs that can overwinter and re-infest the tortoise the following spring.

3. **Variable weather.** In Great Britain and other northern latitude countries spells of good summer weather are regularly interspersed with bouts of cold and often very wet weather. At such times those tortoises outside appear to virtually 'shut down' - they stop feeding and moving around, waiting patiently for the weather to improve. For an adult Herman's tortoise this is a mere inconvenience; for an Egyptian tortoise it could have more serious implications.

4. **Escapes.** Tortoises can be surprisingly agile and are able to climb obstacles quite well; others such as Horsfield's tortoises, are accomplished burrowers and can easily dig their way out of poorly constructed pens. Once out of the pen or garden, recapture of the tortoise may be difficult, as they can be almost impossible to spot once out of their normal home.

5. **Theft.** A combination of the ban on importation and the high cost of both young and adult Mediterranean tortoises mean that there is a thriving illegal market in stolen tortoises. It is best therefore to take reasonable anti-theft precautions (including proof of identification of your tortoises –see Routine Measurements & Records) and not advertising their presence to people that you do not know.

So to build a tortoise enclosure or adapt a pre-existing garden into a tiny portion of the Mediterranean, we need to consider access to sunshine, as this is about the only environmental factor that we cannot easily change or substitute. The garden should be south-facing with full sun falling on to some part of it throughout the day (or at least on those days when it is sunny). This will allow the tortoises to thermoregulate effectively, and they will soon learn the best places to bask at a given time of day. Providing south-facing slopes will help them to do this even more.

In general, housing tortoises in your garden involves either penning the tortoises in away from the garden (and your prize dahlias) or fencing the garden off from your tortoises using low walls or raised beds. There are obviously a variety of ways that one can construct a tortoise pen or to tortoise-proof the garden. Chicken wire or similar is of no use as in some cases it can be climbed or pushed under, and because the tortoise can see beyond the wire there is more incentive for it to try to get past this obstacle. Walls can be constructed from a variety of materials ranging from brick and stone work through to railway sleepers, or even just wooden boards or fencing. Whatever is used it should be solid so that the tortoises cannot see out, and should rise at least 45cm above the ground, preferably with a slight inward overhang. The wall should also extend some 30 cm below the ground level as well to prevent burrowing. Corners should be covered to prevent climbing escapades. Garden gates can be made tortoise-proof by having lift-out boards across the gap that can be stepped over or removed as required.

If a distinct pen is being constructed, then placing a layer of hardcore on to the bottom of the pen before covering with topsoil will not only further reduce the risks of escape by burrowing, but also help to improve the drainage of the pen. Those species such as Horsfield's tortoise will appreciate a dry, rapidly draining substrate such as stony or gravely soil; *T. kleinemanii* are best kept on sand (use silver sand designed for children's sand pits) whilst Herman's tortoise and most of the *T. graeca* complex will enjoy it if there is a 'lawned' area for grazing. Paving stones placed in sunny areas will warm up rapidly and help the tortoise to thermoregulate.

In the wild, many Testudo species will seek out old rodent burrows in which to rest or spend the night. Tortoises appear to regularly return to the same place every evening to spend the night, although this may change occasionally during the course of the year. In captivity provision of shelters is often greatly appreciated, either in the form of semi-natural burrows or even hutches as designed for guinea pigs or rabbits. If you really want to build a tortoise Hilton then consider building a shed or similar with ready access to and from the pen, and install heaters and timed full spectrum lighting for overcast days.

A shallow tunnel allows the tortoise to move from the run to a night time shelter.

Planting can be as imaginative as you like. Many popular garden plants are Mediterranean in origin and will thrive in a sunny, well drained position. Particularly suitable would be plants such as lavender, thyme and rosemary. Encouraging many naturally occurring plants is also important, such as dandelions, sow thistle, plantains and clover. The more the tortoises are able to feed on these 'weeds', the more natural their diet will be. Avoid known or suspected poisonous plants.

Free standing water in a shallow dish should always be available. You may never see your tortoise drink, but it does not mean that it never does.

Pens can be covered by mesh stretched out across a removable frame to help protect your tortoises from potential predators such as magpies.

Basic management of tortoise enclosures involves the regular removal of faeces as soon as seen, as this will help to reduce the risk of parasite build up. Tortoise faeces make an excellent addition to the compost heap. Make sure that you remove any uneaten food daily as this may help to attract rats and other opportunist rodents, and weed out any potentially toxic plants.

Chapter Six

ROUTINE MEASUREMENTS
AND
RECORDS

There are some routine procedures that ought to be performed on each of your tortoises on a regular basis. These are best undertaken twice yearly as a minimum and can easily be incorporated into the routine health checks that are done both before and after hibernation. The before (pre-) hibernation health check should, in the UK, be done in early to mid-September before the tortoise begins to wind down for hibernation. By doing this relatively early it gives us a chance to either sort out minor problems before hibernation, or establish a suitable vivarium if the tortoise is to be kept awake over the winter. The check following (post-) hibernation should be done within two to three weeks after emergence; by this time the tortoise should be eating and drinking and if it is not then further investigations may be required.

These routine checks should include:

1. Weight to length ratio. This is sometimes known as the Jackson ratio after the veterinary surgeon, Oliphant Jackson FRCVS, who first published this simple procedure for *Testudo hermanii* and *T. graeca* see *fig. 1.* and *2.* It is an attempt to gauge the bodily condition of the tortoise by comparing two easily measured factors – its weight and its carapacial length. Where these two values meet is plotted on to a graph that has marked on it two lines. One line is the average weight for length, the second is the minimum acceptable. Tortoises in poor condition will often fall below this line, whilst obese tortoises will be way above the average. For hatchling and young tortoises weight and length checks should be done frequently, for example at monthly intervals, to monitor growth. Many tortoises grow in a series of growth spurts and this may be reflected in your findings. Weight loss is often the first indicator of a problem even if the tortoise appears otherwise well.

Weight: This is measured in grams and if possible is best done on scales that weigh to the nearest gram, although the nearest 5g is acceptable for large tortoises. Do not be afraid to turn your tortoise on its back for the few seconds if it is necessary to get an accurate weight; it will come to no harm.

Length: This is a straight, linear measurement from the most forward point of the carapace to the most hind point. It is not measured over the top of the carapace. If you measure this way then you will get an erroneously long length and the tortoise will appear underweight on the graph.

The weight to length ratio is a useful indicator, but that is all, of a tortoise's physical condition. It is important to bear the following in mind:

   The original work was done on Herman's and Spur-thighed tortoises and is reasonably valid for the species and subspecies of this group. It is not appropriate for *Testudo horsfieldi*, *T. kleinmanni*, *T. marginata* and *Testudo nabulensis*. It probably does not apply to *Testudo whitei*, although it is possible that some may have been included in the original work as mis-identified *T. graeca*. This does not mean that if you have these species you should not bother to take these measurements – in fact quite the contrary because as the years go by this historical information can prove invaluable, particularly if your tortoise becomes unwell. I feel that it is very important to establish such a database of 'normals' for each of your tortoises.

   Male tortoises tend to have a flatter carapace than females, which in turn tend to be more domed. This means that females are often significantly heavier, whilst healthy males can regularly come in either on or just below the 'minimum' line.

2. Overall health check. Give each tortoise a thorough examination, checking not only its shell but its limbs, head, neck and tail for any lesions or, in particular, swellings that may indicate an abscess. Eyes should be bright and there should be no discharge from the eyes, nose or mouth. Your veterinary surgeon will be able to give a more thorough check including an ophthalmic examination.

3. Photocopying or photographing the plastron, to record any changes to keep an up to date record for identification purposes.

4. Worming. As a routine this also works well twice yearly. In particular the post-hibernation worming will help to kill off adult worms before they start producing eggs. Worms are ectotherms too and so as the tortoise begins to thermoregulate and raise its body temperature by basking, so the worms will become active again.

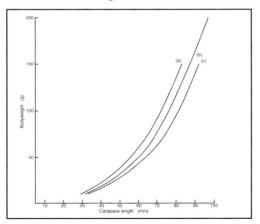
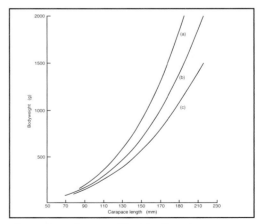

Fig. 1. Growth curve of healthy *Testudo graeca* under 6 months of age showing mass against length. (a(Upper limit; (b) mean; (c) lower limit.

Fig. 2. Growth curve of healthy *Testudo graeca* over 6 months old showing mass against length. (a(Upper limit; (b) mean; (c) lower limit.

O.F. Jackson J. Weight and measurement data on tortoises (*Tesstudo graeca* and *Testudo hermanni*) and their relationship to health. Small Anim. Pract. (1980) 21, 409-416,

Chapter Seven

HIBERNATION

Hibernation in Mediterranean tortoises is a response to low temperatures. As discussed in earlier chapters tortoises are ectotherms that regulate their body temperature by behavioural means. When temperatures drop so low that the tortoise is unable to thermoregulate properly, then most of these tortoises are able to enter a state of dormancy or relative inactivity to see them through this period. However not all Mediterranean tortoises should be hibernated. Those coming from areas that are particularly warm all year around should not be hibernated. They do not do so in the wild and will die if one attempts to hibernate them in captivity.

Species that are safe to hibernate are *Testudo ibera, T whitei, T. marginata, T. hermanii and T. horsfieldi*. Of the *T. g. graeca* group the Moroccan and Algerian races are safe to hibernate.

Species that should **not** be hibernated at all are *T. kleinmanni* and *Testudo nabulensis* (Tunisian tortoises). The Libyan race of *T. g. graeca* should either not be hibernated, or only allowed to do so for a relatively short time, such as six to eight weeks.

Cues for Hibernation

The major cues for triggering hibernation behaviour begin in late summer/early autumn and really begin to come into force following the autumn equinox. These environmental triggers are:
1. Falling ambient temperatures. The days become cooler with lower peak temperatures.
2. Shortening day length. Day length is monitored by the pineal gland.
3. Reduced daylight intensity. The shorter days and lower position of the sun in the sky mean that any sunlight falling on to the tortoise is less intense. This too is monitored by the pineal gland.

Natural Hibernation

During the late spring and summer excess food is converted into fats and sugars and stored in the body. Of particular importance is the substance glycogen (made from blood sugar) that is stored in the liver. Fat is also stored in the liver and other organs.

From mid-September onwards the tortoise's behaviour begins to alter. It will spend longer basking and progressively less time eating. Eventually by late October to early November it will have ceased eating altogether in preparation for hibernation. It will, however, have continued to defaecate and urinate in an effort to eliminate as much waste products from its system as possible.

Once ready for hibernation and guided by the environmental cues the tortoise will either dig into the ground, or select an appropriate shelter (called a hibernaculum) which in the wild is often a vacated rodent burrow. This place is often preselected and the tortoise may return to the same place year after year. It is tempting to think that once underground the tortoise gives up any semblance of thermoregulation but this is not strictly true. The tortoise continues to monitor its surrounding temperature. During the winter as the frost line deepens, so the tortoise will dig deeper to avoid it; as temperatures increase it will dig back up towards the surface.

During hibernation the tortoise is not 'asleep' in the way that we would imagine. The low temperatures mean that their movements are sluggish but they are still responsive to what is going on around them. Also at winter temperatures their whole metabolism is turned down to a minimum setting. Their oxygen requirements are minimal and so little overt breathing is needed, but breathe they must even if it is only occasionally.

Whilst in hibernation the kidneys continue to function, producing small amounts of urine that is stored in the bladder. Because the tortoise rarely urinates during hibernation the natural toxins that are normally eliminated as waste in the urine begin to build up. One such product, urea, can build up to very high levels. This situation is further worsened because the tortoise gradually dehydrates during hibernation. It cannot drink but it does continue to lose tiny amounts of water vapour as it breathes.

Work done with the American Desert tortoise *Gopherus agassizi* found that hibernation killed off the natural gut bacterial flora so that this needed to be established again the following spring (Bjorndal 1987). It is likely that this will also happen in hibernating Mediterranean tortoises.

Re-awakening

The only trigger for hibernation is rising temperatures – these tortoises are underground and so light plays no part in this. Temperatures over around 10°C appear to bring about this 're-awakening'.

To start with the tortoise may just come out and bask for a little while during the day before digging in again at night, but eventually a more normal behaviour pattern is resumed.

Inside the tortoise there is a massive release of glucose from the liver glycogen reserves at this time. This appears to give the tortoise the energy it needs to feed at a time when its body is carrying very high levels of waste in its system. These waste products such as urea can only be eliminated by urinating. This is why tortoises will pass a large urination within days of arousal, and will drink if given the opportunity to rehydrate themselves and flush their kidneys through.

Tortoises should be allowed to drink after hibernation - a cat litter tray makes an excellent bath for this.

Practical Hibernation

Now we've discussed normal hibernation, we can apply that knowledge to hibernating tortoises in captivity. Under normal weather patterns, early November appears to the time in the UK when outside kept tortoises will begin true hibernation. Food should be withheld from around mid-October, or even earlier if the tortoise has access to natural forage. Allowing it to follow a natural feeding pattern is always best. As for hibernation itself, there are several ways that this can be done.

1. Do allow the tortoise to select its own spot in the garden and hibernate at liberty. Relatively dry areas such as under conifers appear to be favourites. This approach has the advantage that the tortoise is in control and there is virtually no input from the owner. The downsides are that there may not truly be any suitable place in your garden. The tortoise will pick the best site that it can but it does not mean that it is perfect. Your tortoise is also potentially at risk from predators such as rodents and natural catastrophes such as floods and gardeners. Tortoises that hibernate outside are very prone to developing shell rot due to

bacterial or fungal infections picked up from the soil.

2. Sinking a bin or other large and deep container into the ground. This is then filled with peat or topsoil. Because the bin is covered the soil inside will be dry and the depth of the bin allows the tortoise to adjust its position according to the soil temperature. This method potentially has lots going for it but the tortoise is still exposed to potential temperature extremes.

3. Indoors in a suitable thermal environment. The ideal temperature for hibernation is around 5-6°C. Above 10°C and the tortoise begins to 'awaken'; below 0°C there is a risk of frost damage. So a suitable place needs to be selected such as an unheated outbuilding. Large refrigerators with the sealing removed from the doors provide ideal conditions for hibernation!

Select a smaller container in which your tortoise is to be hibernated. It can be wooden, plastic or polystyrene and should be large enough for your tortoise to be able to move around in it. This is then filled with a suitable insulator such as polystyrene chips, newspaper or straw (if using straw from a bale please make sure that there is no baler twine mixed in with in – it can wrap around limbs and cause serious problems). This container should have some air holes in the lid. This whole box is placed inside a larger container that also contains insulation material in such a way that all sides of the inner box are insulated. Some air holes should be placed in this box too. There is no need to do hundreds of holes as during hibernation the tortoise's oxygen requirements are minimal and will be easily supplied by twelve or so decent sized ventilation holes. The tortoise will inevitably dig its way to the bottom of

One option for hibernation is to use a polystyrene box packed with shredded paper

the inner box during hibernation; with this arrangement it will still be insulated even if it does so. The insulation material is not keeping the tortoise warm as it does not generate any heat. What it is doing is acting as a buffer against sudden temperature changes outside the box.

Monitor the temperature where the tortoise is stored during the winter. If possible use a max-min thermometer (available from garden supplies) to keep track of temperature variations.

Tortoises should be checked prior to hibernation *(see Routine Measurements and Records)* and their weight recorded because they lose weight during hibernation. On average 1% body weight is lost per month so regular weighing helps you to monitor the tortoise's health during hibernation. Providing the tortoise is not exposed to high temperatures it will not be disturbed from its hibernation by such activities, although they will often hiss whilst being handled. If the weight loss is approaching 8 - 10% then the tortoise must be awakened.

Remember tortoises are not 'asleep' during hibernation and will move around as they would do in the wild, especially if they sense a drop or rise in temperature. This does not mean that they are 'waking up' and should not be taken out of hibernation unless the temperature is correct to do so.

A post-hibernation bath in luke warm water

When temperatures start to rise over 10°C, the tortoise will start to become more active. This is the time to bring it out of hibernation. Give all such tortoises a shallow and warm bath which will allow them to drink and encourage them to urinate. Healthy tortoises should be drinking well within a week of coming out of hibernation and eating within two weeks. If they are not, seek veterinary attention.

Where not to Hibernate

Many owners are concerned about hibernation and believe that there are significant risks involved for their tortoise. Providing the tortoise is of the right species and is healthy, hibernation is a normal thing for these chelonia to do and should be encouraged. The worst possible scenario is to adopt a middle option where the tortoise is 'hibernated' somewhere that is too warm. These tortoises may not be offered food or water (because they're hibernating) or be unwilling to eat or drink because their internal clock says they should be dormant but its just too warm. I've known tortoises to be kept by the Aga in winter (too warm/abnormal day length from kitchen lighting), in bedrooms (too warm/too light) or even in cupboards under the stairs (too warm). In such situations tortoises remain more active then they should and use up vital energy reserves without replacing them by feeding. The naturally occurring dehydration is worsened in these cases too. Such tortoises are more prone to post-hibernation anorexia than those that have been correctly cared for.

Keeping Tortoises Awake through the Winter

Some tortoises such as those listed as inappropriate to hibernate, or those which have been unwell and for whom hibernation may be dangerous, will need to be kept awake throughout the winter. To do this we need a suitable vivarium (see Housing) and we need to reverse the natural environmental cues for hibernation. Ideally we begin this before then autumn equinox and convince the tortoise that it is a Mediterranean summer by providing;
a) High temperatures, with a hot spot that allows the tortoise to achieve a preferred body temperature of 30°C.
b) 14 hours daylight provided by full spectrum lighting. Use two or three tubes to give summer intensity.
   Some tortoises seem to follow their own internal clock no matter what we do. In these cases I would recommend that the tortoise is allowed a short hibernation of four weeks, and is then reawakened and placed in vivarium as described above.

Post-Hibernation Anorexia

Post-hibernation anorexia is when Mediterranean tortoises awakening from hibernation refuse to feed. There are several possibilities as to the cause of this, but typically it is due to inadequate preparation the previous year with insufficient storage of fat. Once the tortoise has used up its entire fat and glycogen reserves (and so also exhausting its fat soluble vitamin stores) it is forced to breakdown muscle and other body proteins as alternative energy and amino acid sources.

Unfortunately this increased protein metabolism causes an increase in urea production which, at a time when levels are naturally high, forces these levels up to dangerous levels. In fact the concentration of urea in the blood stream becomes so high that it suppresses the immune system of the tortoise, depresses appetite and stops the kidneys from working properly. These tortoises have no stored glycogen left to fuel their foraging so their blood sugar levels are very low and so they start on a downward spiral of further protein breakdown leading to higher urea levels and so on. The poor immunity of these animals also leaves them open to secondary bacterial infections especially stomatitis (mouth rot) and septicaemia.

Treatment can be prolonged, and your veterinary surgeon may need to do blood tests and other investigations to find out what is going on inside your tortoise. As a general rule treatment involves:

a) Correcting any dehydration. Initially try regular baths and if after a couple of days the tortoise is not drinking then fluid may need to be given by stomach tube. Use an oral rehydration preparation. This is normally given at around 4% bodyweight per day e.g. if the tortoise weighs 1.0 kg = 1 000g, then 4% would be 40mls that is given divided into 2 or 3 doses each day. It cannot be overstated that correcting the dehydration (which will reduce the blood urea levels and so encourage urination) is crucial to the recovery of the tortoise.

b) Vitamins should be given either by mouth or by injection as the tortoise will have very low levels.

Shell rot affecting the marginal scutes of a *T. graeca* following hibernation buried in the owners garden.

c) Place the tortoise into a vivarium as described for 'keeping tortoises awake'. UVA in particular will help to trigger normal behaviour including feeding. Stomach tube the tortoise with a suitable food replacement. There are now some excellent supportive products available for herbivorous animals such as Critical Care (Oxbow) or Recovery Diet (Supreme Pet Foods) that can be made up into a suspension and tubed. If these are not available then baby foods (vegetable based without milk or milk products) are a useful alternative. Feeding should be done initially twice weekly. In some cases your vet may suggest an indwelling pharyngostomy tube – a tube inserted through the side of the neck and into the stomach with the free end attached to the carapace. It sounds horrendous but it can be very useful, allowing you to feed your tortoise easily and without stress to your tortoise!

d) With the food mix a probiotic. These safe bacterial cultures will help to recolonise the possibly sterile gut of the tortoise helping it towards normal feeding and digestion.

e) Any specific disease conditions, such as stomatitis, should be addressed. Your tortoise should be checked for blindness that can be caused by cataracts. Sometimes these form after exposure to excessively low temperatures during hibernation.

f) Keep going. Some tortoises will take weeks, even months, before they will start to feed normally.

Shell Rot

Tortoises allowed to hibernate outside are particularly prone to this, as organisms in the soil – both bacteria and fungi – invade and establish in the keratin of the scutes. The scutes become pitted and flakey and in some cases the overlying keratin comes away and the underlying bone is exposed. Treatment involves removal of as much of the loose and flakey material as possible and regular cleaning of the affected areas with a topical iodine solution. In the worst cases the infected scutes may need to be removed, often with the tortoise under a general anaesthetic as it can be a very painful procedure, and antibiotics or antifungals may need to be given.

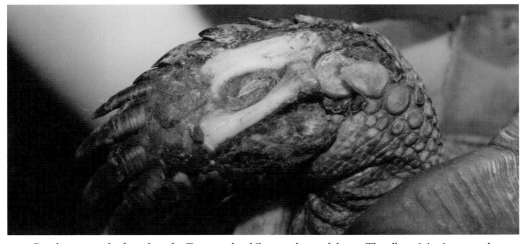

Rat damage to the front leg of a *T.graeca* that hibernated out of doors. The elbow joint is exposed.

Rat damage

Rats and possibly other rodents will gnaw on hibernating tortoises. Typically the outer surfaces of the front legs are damaged as the tortoise draws these legs into

The same tortoise following surgery to clean up the wound and attach a wheel to the plastron. This wheel prevents the tortoise from bearing any weight on the leg, allowing it to heal well.

the shell to protect its head. In severe cases the limb bones and joint may be exposed. Given time and antibiotic cover these can heal well but severe cases may need amputation.

References
Bjorndal K.A. 1987 Digestive efficiency in a temperate herbivorous reptile, Gopherus polyphemus. Copeia 1987 714 –720.

Chapter Eight

REPRODUCTION

Reproduction in Nature

In the wild, the adult females of most of the species of Mediterranean tortoises will lay between one and three clutches of eggs per year. Each clutch will contain between two and twelve eggs on average, the number depending upon the age and size of the female. An exception to this is the Egyptian tortoise *T. kleinmanii*. These females lay only one, occasionally two eggs, at a time. This occurs at monthly intervals until four or five eggs have been laid in total before entering a resting phase of a few months.

The bulk of mating behaviour occurs in the spring, often soon after emergence from hibernation. In male Herman's tortoises the levels of the sex hormones is highest immediately after hibernation, lowering during the main nesting period (April to June) before rising again during the summer – the time of peak sperm production (Huot-Daubremont 2003). In contrast, with females these hormones peaked during the nesting period, but remained high during the summer *during* ovarian activity.

Underside of a male Turkish Spur-thighed tortoise *Testudo g. ibera*. The male has a longer tail than the female and a more beveled plastron

Underside of a female *T.g. ibera*. She has a flat plastron and a much shorter tail.

73

Sexual Behaviour

Sex in tortoises is not as straight forward as it may seem. This is because these reptiles live a relatively solitary existence. Meetings between males and females are relatively scarce and as a result so are opportunities for mating. So within reason, tortoises will mate whenever the opportunity arises and this helps to explain much of their behaviour.

Courtship in tortoises can appear rough - here a male Turkish spur-thighed tortoise heads off a female to prevent her 'escape'.

Male tortoises are sexually promiscuous and will attempt to mate with as many females as possible, whilst driving away other males. By doing so they maximize their chances of fertilizing as many eggs as possible.

Female tortoises that are ready for breeding will appear to play hard to get, often leading the male on a prolonged 'chase'. The male will attempt to butt the female with the front of his plastron and it may be that this, and his ability to keep up with her, allows her to assess his health and strength i.e. his fitness to father her young. Female tortoises are able to store sperm from a single mating for at least several months and so a single mating may provide enough sperm to fertilize several clutches. Eggs are an energetically expensive commodity to produce and so must not be wasted on a second rate male and because mating opportunities are uncommon, it must be with the best she can get when it happens.

Mating itself is a torrid affair. Once a female has accepted a male, he will mount her from behind and attempt to engage his phallus with her cloaca. Female tortoises assist this by extending their back legs to lift their cloaca as far off the ground as possible. In some species this is almost reflex. Female Herman's tortoises will respond to pressure on the back half of the carapace by lifting their back end up. During copulation the male may vocalize – especially Egyptian tortoises with their characteristic bird-like oscillating call.

Egg Laying

In a normal situation males will generally ignore gravid females. The time between mating (and subsequent fertilization) to egg laying is variable because of the ability of the female to store sperm, but can vary from eight weeks to well over two years.

Ovulation – the release of a viable egg from the ovary into the oviduct (the female reproductive tract) – depends upon a number of factors; some internal and some external. Almost certainly the main factor that triggers ovulation is the presence of a sexually active male - especially one that is butting the female and otherwise stimulating her. Pheromones will also play a significant part.

Once in the oviduct the egg is fertilized by a single sperm, and as it descends membranes are added to the egg and finally the calcerous shell is laid down over the outer surface of the egg. Once a clutch of eggs is ready the female will be ready to lay.

Female tortoises select a suitable egg deposition site based upon a number of factors such as soil texture, but the overriding factor is temperature. The surface of the egg deposition site must be warm enough – the female is selecting a place where the eggs are to be incubated at around 25 – 30°C for some eight to twelve weeks. She appears to test the temperature by sniffing the selected area and she may dig several scrapes, again testing the subsurface temperature, with her hind legs first before finally deciding upon the best spot. Some females may not lay their eggs at all if they decide that there is no where suitable to lay. In these cases the eggs just sit in the reproductive tract, eventually causing problems. In some cases extra shells are laid down on these egg, bulking them out to a size where they can no longer be passed.

When egg laying begins the female will scoop out a hole into which each egg is individually laid. Once the clutch is complete, the eggs are covered and the female plays no more part in the care of her eggs or young after this point.

From a practical point of view we need to supply breeding females with suitable nesting conditions. Highfield (2002) suggests that for Mediterranean species these should be:
- A gentle slope, preferably south facing.
- Sandy well drained soil. Often a mixture of play sand (60%) and loamy compost (40%) is accepted.
- Full sun and dry conditions. Mediterranean tortoises will usually lay during the afternoon on warm sunny days.
- Adequate depth of substrate. As a rough guide this should be at least equal to the length of the hind legs plus 70% the length of the carapace.
- For indoor nesting sites these should be around one square metre with the surface heated by a basking lamp.

Reproduction – Related Problems.

Egg-binding

Any female tortoise that shows non-specific signs of ill health, restlessness or persistent straining should be assessed for egg-binding (dystocia). There are two forms:

1 – Pre Ovulatory Ovarian Stasis (POOS). The eggs grow in the ovaries but are

Surgery on a female Herman's tortoise for Pre-Ovulatory Ovarian Stasis (POOS). This is one ovary overloaded with retained yolks.

not ovulated so the ovaries become overloaded with retained yolks. The ovaries form into large pendulous masses which take up a significant amount of space in the body cavity as well as press upon the surrounding organs, causing altered blood flow and other abnormalities. This can be diagnosed either on ultrasound scanning or endoscopy. It may be associated with low thyroid levels. It is also seen in females that have sudden contact with males after often years or even decades without access to other tortoises. Such examples are when owners 'tortoise sit' for other people resulting in two single tortoises being suddenly thrust together. It may be that the physical presence and activity of the male plus pheromones produced by him trigger ovarian activity but full ovulation does not happen.

2 - Post-ovulatory. Here eggs that are shelled to varying degrees are present within the oviducts. It is easily diagnosed by radiography as the shells show up easily. There are many possible causes for this including environmental (no provision of suitable egg deposition sites), low calcium levels, fractured or deformed pelvis, internal tumours and so on so your veterinarian may need to do several tests to investigate this.

Treatment of simple post-ovulatory dystocia involves calcium and oxytocin injections. If these fail to work then removal of the eggs via a surgical flap created in the plastron is advised, possibly accompanied by an ovaro-hysterectomy.

An occasionally reported problem is of eggs smashed whilst still inside the female's body as a result of trauma from matings from hypersexed males. It is thought that the male's phallus cracks the egg shells. Such damage can lead to damage and secondary

This female Herman's tortoise has laid an egg in the surgery following an oxytocin injection. The egg was cracked immediately after laying

infection of the female's reproductive tract.

Prolapsed Phallus

This is where the male is unable to retract his phallus. It becomes progressively damaged by his dragging it along the ground and catching it with his feet. In some cases it can be due to a lack of calcium, in others it is due to damage to the muscle that pulls the phallus back into the cloaca. This damage can occur during mating. Treatment may involve antibiotics and surgical replacement; in others amputation of the phallus is needed. As the male tortoise does not urinate through his phallus this surgery will only affect his ability to mate.

Incubation

Temperature-Dependant Sex Determination

It seems that in all chelonia so far studied, sex determination of embryos is not dependant upon chromosomes as seen in mammals and birds, but appears to be due to the incubation temperature at a critical point of the developmental process.

It appears that at given temperatures certain genes are either switched on or turned off and it is the proteins and enzymes triggered by these genes that eventually lead to the embryo being either male or female. It is still not known to what benefit this is in nature, but in captivity it can be advantageous. By altering the incubation temperature we can skew the proportions of males to females to suit.

As a general rule higher incubation temperatures favour females, whilst lower favours male. In both *T. hermanni* and *T. graeca* temperatures of 25 – 30°C tend to produce males whilst 31 – 35°C generates more females.

Practical Incubation

Tortoise eggs, unlike bird eggs, do not need to be turned so this makes making an incubator relatively straight forward. Commercial reptile incubators and incubator kits are available, but should you wish to make your own then any heat resistant container will do. We obviously need a heat source which can be a small light bulb, a ceramic heater or a vivarium heat mat, connected to an accurate thermostat which has a temperature probe that can be laid next to the eggs. An accurate thermometer is also required, and ideally a hygrometer to measure humidity should be used. These are available from garden centres and specialist reptile outlets. The incubator must not be permanently sealed as some air exchange is necessary even if this is only by lifting the lid once daily to check on the eggs.

The eggs do not need to be buried. Use a small container such as an old clean margarine tub and place some clean sand, earth or vermiculite (available from garden centres) as a substrate into this tub. Then place each egg into the substrate in such a way to create a shallow depression. The eggs should not be touching. Place a card or other label with the species and date of lay in the same tub.

Temperature is crucial, especially with regard to Temperature-Dependant Sex Determination. Humidity less so for hard-shelled Testudo species although an excessively low humidity can lead to drying out of the eggs. As a guide adjust the temperature to 30 - 31°C and aim for a humidity of 70 – 80%.

Incubation Periods for Mediterranean Tortoises

The incubation lengths are guides only as they can vary considerably depending upon the temperature of incubation (lower temperatures produce longer incubation times). In some cases some eggs within a clutch may exhibit diapause, where some eggs show a temporary halt in development, often at the early stages. This may be an adaptive process to stagger the hatching of young over a period of time, possibly to reduce the risk of exposing all of a given brood to unfavorable environmental conditions.

Incubation Periods

Herman's Tortoise	*(Testudo hermanni)*		75 - 80 days at 25 - 28°C
		or	56 - 63 days at 30 - 31°C
Spur-thighed tortoise	*(Testudo graeca)*		75 - 80 days at 25 - 26°C
		or	56 - 63 days at 30 - 31°C
Spur-thighed tortoise	*(Testudo graeca ibera)*	around	56 - 65 days at 30°C
Marginated tortoise	*(Testudo marginata)*		75 - 80 days at 25 - 26°C
		or	56 - 63 days at 30 - 31°C
Egyptian tortoise	*(Testudo kleinmanni)*		80 - 111 days at 30 - 33°C
Horsfield's tortoise	*(Testudo horsfieldi)*		61 - 75 days at 30 - 31°C

Apparent Infertility

Adult tortoises may be infertile for a variety of reasons, but sometimes their eggs do not develop because the nutrition of the adults is poor. Work on Herman's tortoise eggs (Speake et al 2001) suggests that yolks are low in docosahexaenoic acid and vitamin A levels (both essential for the developing embryo). So adult diets low in these substances, or in their precursors of alpha-linolenic acid and beta-carotene will result in insufficiencies in the yolks and failure of the tortoise embryos to develop. Feeding red, yellow or orange vegetables such as carrot or peppers will help with these.

Failure to Hatch/Dead-in-Shell

There are many reasons why tortoise eggs do not hatch. In the first instance consider the following:
1. Temperature. Temperatures too high or too low can lead to embryonic death
2. Humidity. Tortoise eggs are relatively resistant to poor humidity levels; this is probably why so many people have managed to hatch eggs in airing cupboards. However it should be monitored and if possible a humidity of 70 - 80% maintained. A very low humidity or a high airflow over the eggs can lead to an excessive loss of water from the eggs leading to dehydration and embryonic death. An egg that loses 25% or more of its weight during incubation is unlikely to hatch.
3. Oxygen and carbon dioxide levels. Remember that a developing tortoise inside the egg does breathe – not through its lungs but across the egg shell. On the inside of the shell are membranes well supplied with blood vessels that pick up oxygen through microscopic holes in the shell and disperse carbon dioxide the same way. In sealed incubators or containers housed inside larger incubators oxygen levels may fall and carbon dioxide levels rise to dangerous levels. Briefly opening such incubators once daily or every other day will prevent this from happening.

Once an egg is laid and has come to rest, the embryo (which at this stage consists of only an aggregate of cells), gradually migrates up to the highest point of the shell so that it eventually comes to sit on top of the yolk. After 24 to 48 hours it attaches to the inner cell membrane - the allantois. This membrane is important for oxygen uptake and carbon dioxide release, calcium absorption from the shell and storage of harmful waste products. This connection is essential but is, to start with, very fragile. Any rotation of the egg within the period of 24 hours after laying to around 20 days of incubation is liable to sheer off the embryo and cause its subsequent death.

When handling eggs always be careful not to rotate them. When removing eggs from natural egg sites to place into incubators always try to do it within 24 hours of laying and mark the top of each egg with a permanent marker pen or similar so that you always know which way is up.

Candling

Candling is a means of attempting to find out if eggs are fertile. It involves shining a very bright light through the egg. If there is a sizeable embryo present it will be seen as a shadow. Often such a shadow is not visible until almost the end of incubation – possibly because it is only by this point that the developing tortoise is dense enough to block any light.

Hatching

As incubation progresses the shell becomes thinner in patches as calcium is absorbed from the outer calcified layer and incorporated into the developing tortoise. Eventually the tortoise will hatch. There is a small "egg tooth" on the nose of the hatchling tortoise, and it uses this to wear its way through the shell until it begins to crack. Often once the shell is punctured and a small chip is displaced, then the tortoise may take a rest.

Eventually the tortoise will be able to climb out of the shell, a perfect miniature of the adult. Many will appear to be bent over – a necessity inside the confines of the egg. Over the next twenty four hours or so they will gradually straighten out.

Occasionally some hatching tortoises will appear to have trouble getting out of their shell. It is tempting to help them out of their shell but be careful. These hatchlings often have large yolk sacs still that have not been absorbed, and the blood vessels lining the inside of the shell are still functional. It is very easy to damage these structures with a serious risk of haemorrhage or wounding.

Aftercare

These newly hatched tortoises still have a yolk sac internally to supply them with food for the first few days. However it is better to offer food sooner rather than later. Feed shredded pieces of green foods plus a calcium supplement. Also bathe the tortoise every day to encourage it to drink.

Hatchling tortoises need to be kept in vivaria. The advice discussed under *Housing* should be implemented, but of particular importance is the provision of hiding places. Hatchling and young tortoises have many predators in the wild

Bady tortoises such as these six month old *T. ibera* need to be kept in an appropriate vivaria.

so instinctively they appreciate cover, behaviour that will also lead them into appropriate microclimates that help them to survive. Make sure that you provide these and the chances are that your well-adjusted baby tortoises will soon learn where the food comes from and will readily greet you at the front of their vivarium.

References

Highfield A.C 2002 **Natural and Artificial Nest sites for Terrestrial Tortoises** *in* Tortoise Trust Newsletter Number 3 & 4 pp 19 - 20

Huot-Daubremont C, Bradshaw SD, Bradshaw FJ, Kuchling G, and Grenot CJ (2003) **Variation of plasma sex steroid concentrations in wild and captive populations of Hermann's tortoise (Testudo hermanni hermanni) in Southern France.** *in* Gen Comp Endocrinol. Feb; 130(3):299-307

Speake BK, Surai PF, and Gore M (2001) **Lipid composition, fatty acid profiles, and lipid-soluble antioxidants of eggs of the Hermann's tortoise (Testudo hermanni boettgeri)** *in* Zoo Biol 20:75-87, 2001.

Chapter Nine

TORTOISE HEALTH

Tortoises are relatively hardy animals providing they are healthy and well cared for. However, as with all animals, some do become ill for a variety of reasons.

Tortoises that are ill are best kept in vivaria where their environment can be controlled appropriately. Ideally this should be hygienic – use only newspaper on the bottom so that it can be cleaned out readily, and make sure that any vivarium furniture such as hides can either be sterilized or thrown away. In addition to this the basic care for an unwell tortoise should include the following:

1. Provision of a stress free environment.
2. Provide an appropriate temperature. The preferred body temperature of Testudo species is around 30°C. If kept at too low a temperature their immune system will not function. In *Testudo g. ibera* there is no antibody production below 10°C. If the tortoise is on medication such as antibiotics, keeping it at its preferred body temperature will mean that its body manages and eliminates the drug in a manner predictable to your veterinary surgeon.

A female *T. graeca* anaesthetised and ready for surgery.

3. Keeping the tortoise well hydrated is essential. Daily baths are a good way of achieving this. The water should be luke-warm and filled up the junction between the carapace and the plastron. Bathing allows the tortoise to drink easily and often encourages it to defaecate and urinate.

Stomach tubing is a useful nursing technique for giving fluids to dehydrated individuals or certain medications such as wormers. Use a flexible plastic or silicon tube attached to a syringe. The length of tube is measured by placing it against the plastron of the tortoise. The correct length is from the tip of the gular scute to the hinge between the abdominal and femoral scutes. Mark the required length on the tube. The technique is as follows:

a) Lubricate the tube with KY Jelly or vegetable oil.

b) To insert the tube hold the tortoise vertically with its head uppermost. It is easier if there is a second person to hold the tortoise's front legs back as it will try to push you away.

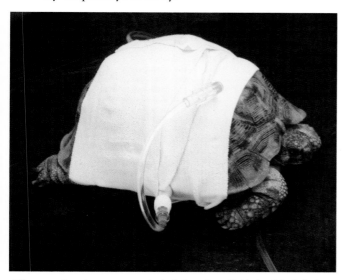
The same female post-operatively being given fluids by drip infusion into the bone of the shell.

c) Pull the head out from the shell until the neck is reasonable straight. Easy to say but difficult to do as large tortoises have very strong neck muscles.

d) With your index finger press firmly but gently against the lower jaw and pull it down away from the upper. Often the quicker this is done the easier it is.

Place your index finger into the angle of the jaw so that it acts as a gag. Most tortoises will not bite down on it. Gently insert the tube into the back of the mouth by running it along the roof of the mouth.

This way you avoid the wind pipe at the back of the tongue.

With the head stretched out, once the mark is reached the tip of the tube should be nicely in the stomach. Depress the plunger slowly to empty the syringe's contents.

Monitor the back of the mouth – if any fluid comes up from the oesophagus then stop.

If in doubt use only small volumes. The stomach is not huge in tortoises so give no more than 10mls of fluid to a large tortoise of 2.0kg or more.

Infectious Diseases

Runny Nose Syndrome (RNS): RNS is a common and often debilitating disease seen in tortoises. However there appears to be no single cause of RNS. Infectious agents associated with RNS include chelonian herpesvirus and mycoplasmas (see under individual headings), but in some cases RNS can be linked to general poor health or problems that are not immediately obvious, such as an internal abscess. An investigation into RNS may involve submitting nasal discharge for laboratory investigation to look for chelonid herpes virus and mycoplasma DNA, bacteriological culture as well as blood samples and radiographs.

It is thought that *Testudo graeca ibera* may be an asymptomatic carrier of at least one infectious agent of RNS, with deaths in mixed collections being mostly confined to the North African Spur-thighed tortoise *Testudo g.graeca*.

Viral Diseases

Chelonian Herpesvirus: This is a serious viral disease of all terrestrial chelonia and is a common cause of Runny Nose Syndrome. Until recently this virus could only be diagnosed with either virus isolation from tissue or nasal mucus – a process frequently yielding poor results, or by histological study of a liver biopsy. Now there is a test available that identifies herpesvirus DNA in samples that should prove to be a more sensitive and accurate test.

Tortoises with RNS show a persistent rhinitis, with a nasal discharge that can vary from clear and watery to thick and mucoid. There appears to be an accompanying immunosuppression and affected tortoises often have recurring parasitic infestations (especially with flagellates). Appetite generally remains good but

A male *T. graeca* showing the surgical repair of the plastral flap needed to allow a liver biopsy to be taken.

84

diarrhoea is often a feature. In some cases it progresses and the tortoise can become anaemic. Other organs such as the liver and the tongue lining can become involved. These tortoises can become jaundiced. Death can follow often as a result of a secondary stomatitis, pneumonia or kidney failure. Treatment with the human anti-herpesvirus medication acyclovir has been suggested but not proven as an effective medication.

Iridovirus: This may be an up and coming viral infection and evidence of it is often found in red blood cells of sick tortoises. It has been linked to mortalities although this has not been proven.

Bacterial Diseases

Abscesses are very common in tortoises. Reptilian pus is rarely liquid but is more often thick, cheese-like material. A thick fibrous capsule usually surrounds the abscess making antibiotic penetration difficult, so surgery is often resorted to to effect a cure. Where limbs, joints or extremities such as the nose are affected, then radiography should be performed to check for osteolysis in the underlying bone.

Tympanic: (ear) abscesses are common, and show as bulging of the tympanic scale on one or both sides. These are often secondary to a bacterial stomatitis, with infection ascending the eustachian tube into the middle ear cavity. Management

A male *T. ibera* with head tilt due to an infection in the brain.

of all abscesses is similar, involving the combination of appropriate antibiotics and surgical removal of pus.

Stomatitis: (or mouth rot) is occasionally encountered especially following hibernation. There may be ulcerative, haemorhagic lesions or whitish plaques on the tongue, back of the mouth and hard palate. Bacterial infections usually play a significant role, although viral and fungal causes have been implicated. Following swabbing for routine bacterial culture, cleaning it up under a general anaesthetic is recommended. Antibiotics or antifungals should be used depending upon the cause. Chelonia with stomatitis will not eat or drink voluntarily.

Septicaemia: presents as haemorrhages in the skin and in the shell. In severe cases fluid may accumulate beneath the keratin shields of the shell. Jaundicing may be seen. Antibiotics and fluid support is essential in these cases.

Salmonella: There is often concern about the risk of contracting Salmonella from tortoises, but infections from chelonia are relatively rare and are usually due to a breakdown in hygiene and poor husbandry, allowing an environmental build up.

Mycoplasmas: These are bacteria-like organisms that cause inflammation of the nasal cavity and around the eyes producing a typical RNS picture. Symptoms are similar to that seen with Chelonid Herpesvirus. Infection can be long term and in some individuals no symptoms may be visible.

Fungal Diseases

Although most "shell rot" in terrestrial chelonia are bacterial, occasionally fungal infections are seen. These are more of a "dry rot". Treat by debridement, topical povidone-iodine and anti-mycotics.

Parasites

Flagellate infestations can be associated with gastro-intestinal disease and a loss of appetite in chelonia, which may be seen to void large quantities of watery diarrhoea. Examination of faeces under a light microscope will reveal huge numbers of these motile protozoa. They are considered a normal inhabitant of the gut fauna, but in large numbers they are pathogenic. In many cases they are secondary opportunists so the possibility of a concurrent disease should be considered. Treat with metronidazole delivered by stomach tube at 100-275mg/kg once only. Occasionally the protozoan Hexamita may be a cause of kidney disease.

Worms

Around 30-40% of tortoises carry nematode infestations, usually Tachygonetria species. Other species found include Sulcascaris and Angusticaecum. Tachygonetria worms are particular parasites of Testudo species. Several different species can be found living naturally in the intestine of wild tortoises and it is thought that here they may be beneficial, helping to churn over the gut contents and break it down to aid bacterial degradation. In captivity however any stress on the tortoise such as poor diet or living conditions can tip the balance in favour of the worms triggering problems. Large infestations will compete for the host's food, and can cause blockages.

Angusticaecum are large worms. The larval stages undergo a migration through the body's tissue and can cause pathology in a variety of organ systems. Life cycles are believed to be indirect though they have not been worked out - Angusticaecum can have a direct life cycle. Eggs can survive for months and certainly overwinter outside to re-infect the tortoise the following spring. Regular worming with fenbendazole at 50 to 100mg/kg bodyweight or oxfendazole at 68mg/kg twice yearly is to be recommended. This is best undertaken during pre- and post-hibernation checks.

A common situation that appears to arise is where owners gradually accumulate a number of tortoises over successive years. During this period worm numbers and the egg burden in the soil builds up to such a level where worms become an obvious problem, often seen in the faeces and occasionally inside the mouth. In such cases there can appear to be a sudden and mysterious appearance of worms. They have not come in from outside, on food or in birds but have just passed a numerical threshold where their presence becomes obvious.

Fly strike

Occasionally maggots may be seen after flies have laid eggs on faecal-stained areas especially around the cloaca. These should be removed as quickly as possible and the area cleaned up with an iodine based wash. Seek veterinary attention as soon as possible.

Ticks

Are rarely encountered except on wild caught chelonia. They ought to be removed individually. Be aware that abscesses can arise at tick attachment sites.

Note: The parasiticide Ivermectin should never be used with tortoises as it regularly causes fatalities.

Non-infectious Diseases

Most of the common non-infectious diseases such as nutritional problems have been dealt with in other chapters.

Diseases of the Urinary System

Gout. Tortoises eliminate most of their waste nitrogen as uric acid and this is seen as the white crystals typical of normal urine. In cases of kidney disease or severe dehydration, where uric acid is not voided with the urine, it can crystallize out in the kidneys causing serious renal damage. Uric acid crystals can also form in other organs and joints as well causing the condition known as gout. This is a serious condition and can prove fatal. Gout is a common consequence of many disease processes in tortoises because once the tortoise stops eating and drinking there is an ever increasing risk of gout being triggered.

Bladder stones

Are a particular problem with young tortoises. Often it is as a result of prolonged mild dehydration such as seen where the tortoises do not have access to a humid microclimate (under branches or hides). Uric acid crystals form in

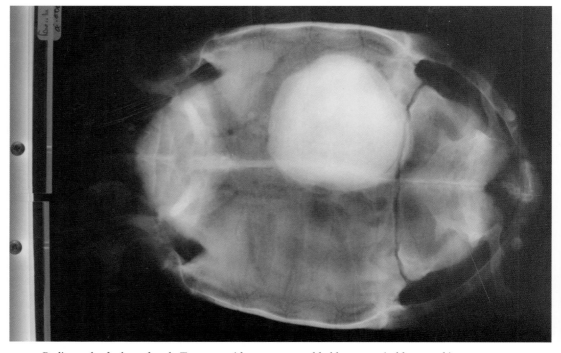

Radiograph of a large female *T. graeca* with an enormous bladder stone visable as a white mass.

the bladder and these attract more until a stone is formed. These stones can act as a focus for infection and cause a cystitis. Often these are passed out, with some straining on the part of the tortoise. In others the bladder stone is too big to be passed out and surgery may be needed, or medication in the form of allopurinol to stop the further formation of more uric acid. Bladder stones usually show up well on radiographs.

Drowning

Tortoises can and do fall into unprotected ponds and streams. The position of the lungs in the top part of the carapace means that they can survive for some time, but should this happen to your tortoise you must seek immediate veterinary attention. First of all however try working the limbs of the tortoise in and out of the shell to compress the lungs, whilst holding the tortoise upside down. This may help to void excess water from the lungs. Tortoises submerged for long periods of time take on large volumes of water and diuretics may need to be administered to help the tortoise eliminate this excess. Inhalation of water will lead on to pneumonia so antibiotics are often needed.

Chapter Ten

LEGISLATION

The main piece of legislation affecting tortoises worldwide is The Convention on the International Trade in Endangered Species of Flora and Fauna (CITES). The operative words are *'trade in'*. In the European Union species are listed as either Annex A or Annex B.

Annex A covers those species where only trade in captive bred animals is permitted and it is tightly controlled. No specimens can be taken from the wild for commercial purposes.

For Mediterranean tortoises the Annex A species are:

Testudo marginata
Testudo kleinmanni
Testudo hermanii
Testudo werneri
Testudo graeca

This list would include all subspecies, geographic races and those newer species such as Gilbert White's tortoise (*T. whitei*) and *Testudo nabulensis* which were previously covered under the *T. graeca* complex.

Annex B. This covers all other tortoises, including Horsfield's tortoise (*T. horsfeldi*).

Specifically in the UK, the sale of those tortoises listed under Annex A requires certification from the Department of the Environment, Food and Rural Affairs (DEFRA). The certificate that is required is an Article 10.

An Article 10 certificate constitutes one of the following:

The Leopard tortoise (*Geochelone pardalis*) is commonly available in the pet trade It is a large species that requires tropical temperatures and should not be hibernated. This tortoise species is found in sub-Saharan Africa

The Background yellow colour plus the dark, blotch-like pattern give the
Leopard tortoise its distinctive name.

a) Specific Specimen Certificate. This is issued for a tortoise that is permanently identified. This means that it has been micro chipped. Describing visible characteristics will not suffice. This certificate accompanies an individual tortoise throughout its life and should be passed on to the new owner if the tortoise is sold.

b) Transaction Certificate. This will be issued if the tortoise is too small to be micro chipped (or if it is a very rare specimen). This certificate covers one transaction only. If the tortoise is to be resold then a new Transaction Certificate needs to be obtained.

Two more things must be noted:

The sale of Annex B species does not require certification. For our purposes this only applies to Horsfield's tortoise.

Giving away an Annex A species, for example as a gift or to a tortoise charity, does not require an Article 10. However I would always strongly recommend that with each transfer of a tortoise a letter handing over ownership to the new owner should be supplied.

The sale of an Annex A tortoise without appropriate certification is illegal in the UK. For further guidance please look at www.ukcites.gov.uk and seek out the section on *Guidance Notes for Tortoise Traders (GN3)*. For countries other than the UK please seek advice from the local authorities so that you comply with any legislation.

Microchipping

This involves the insertion of a microchip transponder into the tortoise so as to permanently identify the individual. In the UK the recommended site is in the left thigh. At present it can only be legally performed by a veterinary surgeon as the hole left in the relatively inelastic tortoise skin does require closure – either by suture or tissue glue.

Tortoises of carapace length less than 10cm are considered too small for microchipping.

Baby Leopard tortoises are appealing....

...but with good care they can grow into seriously big tortoises!

Plastron Photocopying

Another way of identifying your tortoise is to regularly photocopy the plastron.

The red-foot tortoise (*Geochelone caronaria*) is another species from tropical climes - this time South America. This species should have a significant amount of fruit in its diet.

The Indian tortoise (*Geochelone elagans*) is another species that is occasionally encountered. This species is a native of India, Sri Lanka and Pakistan and so needs a warm (background temperature of 22°C to 26°C with a hotspot up to 36°C) and humid environment. This baby will have an eventual carapace length of around 25cm.

Each tortoise has a unique plastron and can be identified by it. This means of identifying individuals is not appropriate for CITES purposes.

93

Index

94